THE ITALIAN ECONOMY

WORLD ECONOMIES

A series of concise modern economic histories of the world's most important national economies. Each book explains how a country's economy
works, why it has the shape it has, and what distinct challenges it faces.
Alongside discussion of familiar indicators of economic growth, the coverage extends to well-being, inequality and corruption, to provide a fresh and
more rounded understanding of the wealth of nations.

PUBLISHED

Matthew Gray
THE ECONOMY OF THE GULF STATES

Vera Zamagni
THE ITALIAN ECONOMY

The Italian Economy

Vera Zamagni

agenda
publishing

First edition published in 2018 by Agenda Publishing

Agenda Publishing Limited
The Core
Bath Lane
Newcastle Helix
Newcastle upon Tyne
NE4 5TF

www.agendapub.com

ISBN 978-1-911116-77-6 (hardcover)
ISBN 978-1-911116-78-3 (paperback)

British Library Cataloguing-in-Publication Data
A catalogue record for this book is available from the British Library

Typeset by Patty Rennie
Printed and bound in the UK by TJ International

Contents

Preface

The Italian economy today does not enjoy a good press and gets very poor ratings from international agencies. There are two main reasons for this. Over the short run, this has been a consequence of the world financial crisis, which has hit Italy much harder than other countries. In 2007, Italy's per capita income was 107 (with the European Union average = 100), while France's stood at 108, Germany's at 117, the UK's at 111, and Spain's at 103. In 2016, the respective positions were: Italy 96, France 105, Germany 123, UK 108, Spain 92, which shows that only Germany, among the biggest of the EU countries, has overcome the crisis, while the other countries have lost percentage points, with Italy and Spain the most severely affected. This book will offer plenty of arguments to explain the grim performance of Italy since the crisis, while also explaining why Italy is still in the G7, why it is still one of the largest economies of the EU and still remains a major exporter of manufactured goods, despite having lost 25 per cent of its manufacturing production since the crisis, chiefly as a result of a major shrinking of its domestic market.

Secondly, and more profoundly, over the long-run the Italian economy has never fitted the standard US growth models based on big business, standardization, economies of scale and transnationalism. Although this lack of fit did not prevent the country from modernizing and growing, it did result in a vast underevaluation of the Italian economy by international bodies that often left Italy out of international comparisons or alternatively negatively commented upon, even when it performed well. Some years ago *The Economist* compared the Italian economy to the leaning tower of Pisa suggesting that it was always on the brink of falling to pieces. One could point out that Pisa's tower has been standing for seven centuries, and was recently consolidated so that it cannot fall down, at least for the foreseeable future and can be safely visited by masses of people. However, the image of fragility is the one that circulates: Italy as a country that cannot be relied upon, because it is not "stable" or "sustainable", both politically and economically.

It is true to say that inside the predominant Anglo-Saxon economic approach Italy is not at ease and strives to find ways of flourishing without fully embracing it, a very uncomfortable position. The reason for this stems from its historical roots, which have moulded an economy as a place of small businesses, territorial specificities, small cities, relational skills, quality products and a proudly cultivated natural and cultural biodiversity. In a world in which huge transnational corporations and worldwide platforms tend to produce uniformity, Italian diversity is not a winning card.

This book sets out to show how history – a remarkably long history – is still shaping the Italian present and how Italy tries to compete in this world without discarding it, as many developing countries have done, losing much of their identity in the process. Chapter 1 summarizes the most important legacies of the past, a history that has left lasting marks not on Italy alone, but on the entire world. I maintain that any flourishing of the Italian economy after periods of decline entails a reworking of the past, rather than its demise and that to understand the postwar Italian economy an historical approach is necessary. In Chapter 2 I examine the years, 1945–2016, and use a periodization that fits with actual stages of Italy's economic development. Chapter 3 presents an overall quantitative picture of the evolution of the Italian economy in the postwar period, and is articulated in appropriate sub-periods, including an examination of demography, economic growth, employment, productivity, income, public administration, the welfare state, finance, monetary issues and institutions. The international position of the country and the important regional differentiation within it, especially the North–South gap, are covered. Chapter 4 gets to the heart of the Italian economy, where the specific form of the Italian productive system, based on small and medium-sized enterprises (SME), is explained in detail, as well as the large presence of cooperatives and non-profit organizations and the importance of tourism. The vast array of SMEs show a strong tendency to build networks to support competitiveness – an alternative to economies of scale. Finance and banking sectors are also discussed.

The final two chapters are devoted to a more extended treatment of human and social factors, exploring such topics as migration, organized crime and the strength of civil society. The book ends by reminding that Italy is among those few countries that still invest in community-based development, respecting regional traditions and promoting local cultures to attain public well-being, inclusiveness and social cohesion. It is not only Italian civil society that is supportive of this approach, but also the many successful SMEs, which are an expression of the regions where they are located and which base their success on the support of such regions, as well as on their openness to the world. As I have said, the Italian style is not the predominant approach of business today, but there are reasons to believe that it will be increasingly appreciated for its quality of life appeal, as long as the world still hosts biodiversity not only in products and services, but in the very processes of production and in the general aims of economic activity.

This volume derives from my extensive studies of Italian economic history since the unification of the country – with special reference to the standard of living, the role of the state, business history, and social enterprises – and embodies the work of many colleagues with whom I have shared research projects and I have co-authored publications. My thanks go to all of them. I also owe much to the many students of the Italian universities where I have taught and to the generations of international students of the SAIS Europe Centre of the Johns Hopkins University, where I have been a professor since returning from Oxford in 1973 after obtaining my doctorate. Their curiosity and intellectual stimuli have prevented me from considering any attainment as a final target.

I dedicate this book to my husband Stefano, life companion, intellectual inspiration, and above all passionate testimonial to an interpretation of academic life that is at the service of progress of society, which sustains hard work, launches new intellectual adventures and nurtures the hope that it is possible to improve the lot of every person.

V Z

Bologna

NOVEMBER 2017

Tables and Figures

TABLES

FIGURES

Modern day Italy showing regions and cities

1

Introducing the Italian economy

The Italian economy is generally included today as part of the "periphery" of Europe alongside other Mediterranean countries. This might give a correct picture of its relative economic position at the beginning of the twenty-first century, but it conceals the fact that Italy has played a central role in Europe for very long stretches of time over the last two millennia and a half. To understand Italy today one must keep in mind two historical strands: a far from brilliant present and the legacy of a glorious past, which lives not only in the immense artistic heritage concentrated in this very small country (300,000 square kilometres), but in its living scientists, businessmen, artists, sportsmen and in the very character of its people and its communities. Italy is a country of contrasts, hosting side by side examples of excellence and signs of retardation, in a social context that is capable of ensuring their unlikely coexistence.

The aim of this chapter is to highlight the most important components of this legacy from a past that has made Italy a unique place in the world: a country having experienced three quite different civilizations: Roman, the city-states/Renaissance, and the modern industrial age, alternating with two declines. In the first two civilizations, Italy was a leader, in the last a follower of only partial success. The Italian past is not simply a historical memory – it has left important marks on the urban, economic, cultural and social structure of the country that are visible today.

1

THE ROMANS

We have evidence of the presence of man in the Mediterranean peninsula, later called Italy, from the Paleolithic era (1.5 million years ago). Its position at the centre of the Mediterranean Sea made the Italian peninsula with its surrounding islands a crossroads for Indo-European peoples, mixing local inhabitants and newcomers and forming settlements. Among them, the Etruscans (who inhabited the region later called Tuscany) developed a sophisticated civilization between the eighth and sixth century BCE along the Tyrrhenian part of Italy, federating several cities, including the villages that were later to form Rome. Sicily and Sardinia hosted Phoenician settlements and in the south of the peninsula and in Sicily there were Greek settlements. In the eighth century BCE the villages of the central part of the Tyrrhenian coast proclaimed a kingdom with Rome as its capital. The inhabitants organized the new state and built an army to defend it from its neighbours. According to ancient accounts, Rome had seven kings, before becoming a republic around 500 BCE, with a collegial form of governance, which was to come to include representation from the lower classes (hence the famous slogan *Senatus Populusque Romanus* – SPQR – "the Senate and People of Rome", which conveys the idea of two institutions jointly governing the republic, the senate and popular assembly).

During the republican period, the Romans first unified southern Italy, defeating the Greek army, before embarking on a long and difficult confrontation with the Phoenicians (from northern Africa, having their capital in Carthage), that finally ended with victory and Rome's control of the western Mediterranean. In the second century BCE, Rome completed its defeat of Greece, hegemonizing part of the eastern Mediterranean, before commencing the conquest of the northern peoples of continental Europe (the Gauls and the Istrians). All of these conquests were achieved by a republican government, despite the increasing difficulties of exercising control over such a vast territory. Despite reforms that included the extension of Roman citizenship to the other peoples of the Italian peninsula (later Roman citizenship was further extended beyond the peninsula) and the improvement of the conditions of its slaves, the survival of the Republic was jeopardized by civil war among its leaders until the de facto transition to an authoritarian government with Rome's first emperor, Augustus in 31 BCE. However, the Senate remained in place until the sixth century CE, albeit with different prerogatives, and the position of emperor was not automatically inherited and could be appointed by the Senate.

The Roman Empire came to encompass the entire Mediterranean coast and the northern European belt including England, becoming truly multi-ethnic. In the fourth century CE it was forced to defend its borders, and in the fifth century it partitioned into eastern and western parts. The western part was later conquered by the northern peoples (generically called barbarians because of their more primitive societal organization), who deposed the last Roman Emperor in 476, while the eastern part, centred on Constantinople (or Byzantium) lasted until 1453, when it was finally conquered by Ottoman Turks, who built the Ottoman Empire on its ashes.

This brief history of the milennial Roman Empire shows that it did not resemble other empires in one important respect: it had lived for centuries as a republic practicing shared power and when it became an empire it was not as absolute as others because of the continued presence of the Senate and the diffusion of Christianity, which was first seen as a challenge to authority and then became organized as a separate power. Civil society in the Roman state always had the opportunity to organize and to have a voice. Against this background the Romans were able to develop an extremely important body of legislation – collected in 529–34 by Justinian (the last eastern Roman Emperor) in the *Corpus Iuris Civilis* – that became the basis of all later European legislations. The necessity to balance powers, the readiness to grant citizenship to different peoples, the need to produce a well-established order that could be observed everywhere, were powerful incentives to use the legislative instruments creatively, fixing rules in codes that could be applied universally based on general principles rather than simply on local customs or religions.

Amid their conquests, the Romans assimilated philosophical, scientific and artistic contributions from many peoples, to which they added their own contributions. Alongside law, they excelled in engineering and architecture. Aqueducts, dams, amphitheatres, sewers, thermal baths, public and private palaces built in stone, temples, basilicas, roads, bridges, arches, domes and public toilets were built across the Roman state, bequeathing to its cities a way of living that was indeed the best of the time. The city of Rome hosted up to one million inhabitants and several other Italian cities were of substantial size. In technological innovation the Romans eclipsed their contemporaries, with the use of water mills, concrete, cranes, agricultural machinery, metal leagues, pumps, skew presses, looms, rudders, new types of sails, glass and mirrors. Even the principle of the steam engine was known to them, although never used for productive purposes. Military technology and logistics became increasingly sophisticated, not only in the strategies of deploying infantry and cavalry in the ways most appropriate to different battlefields, but also in the use of machines during sieges and the capability to build encampments and structures to allow rapid mobilization (carriages, boats, bridges).

After having lasted around a thousand years, the Roman state collapsed, invaded by peoples from continental Europe (mostly Germanic), who came to rule its former territories without stable government and amidst continued conflict with Byzantium, leading to general destruction and civil decline. In the eighth century the Franks appeared in Italy and a century later the Arabs arrived, creating further instability. What happened next in Italy was an unanticipated reversal of fortune.

THE FLOURISHING OF THE CITY-STATES AND THE RENAISSANCE

Taking advantage of the chaos in which the Italian peninsula had plunged, some of the early cities slowly rebuilt themselves and, being distant from an established power, they developed an original form of self-government that proved instrumental to the birth of the modern economy, science and art. Beginning in the eleventh century, the coastal cities (Genoa, Pisa,

Amalfi, Nola, Gaeta, Venice, Ancona) that were able to develop trade as the Mediterranean Sea had become safer, and some of the cities of the centre-north that had been in existence in the Roman period (including Milan, Verona, Bologna, Florence, Siena, but also many other smaller ones) became self-governed republics, a form of government which had not been unknown in the country, and made freedom (*libertas*) their flag. While the independence of the communes in the south did not last long – the area was unified by foreign rule (first by the French, later by the Spanish) in alliance with the local landed aristocracy – the communes of north and central Italy had long lives as independent city-states. The efforts by foreign powers to end their independence were successfully resisted and foreign dominance came only some centuries later, allowing the Italian city-states the time to flourish economically and artistically, in spite of the countless conflicts between them to acquire more land and exert control over neighbouring communes.

The city of Rome had a separate destiny. Since the sixth century it had slowly fallen under the administration of the Christian papacy, in conjunction with local aristocratic families. Territorial donations from the conquests of various kings and barons enabled the pope to gradually enlarge the papal controlled lands, which would eventually become a true papal state in the sixteenth century, and which would last until the unification of Italy itself. As the home of the Holy See, the city of Rome witnessed the building of beautiful churches, palaces, squares, monuments and parks, but never developed economically along the mercantile lines of the other Italian city-states.

The urban shape of these Italian cities clearly conveys the idea of shared governance of a place, with a central square devoted to a market, festivals and celebrations. Facing the main square were the public palaces – the cathedral, the municipal palace, the guildhall – and from the central square the main streets led away to the private palaces of merchants and aristocratic families, to the houses and workshops of artisans, to convents, hospitals and other churches. Protective walls were raised, and often enlarged to accommodate more people and more activity. Buildings were built in stone and brick (not wood), explaining the longevity of architecture in these cities.

The civilization born out of these city-states was a consequence of the institutions that made self-government viable and of the wealth that was accumulated in them. Table 1.1 details comparative estimates of per capita income in Europe 1000–1600 and shows the rise of north-central Italy above any other area of Europe. It also shows the growth over the period of the low countries (Holland), which imitated the Italian city-states by creating its own republic, while England lagged behind and Spain, Portugal, France and Germany were never in a position to catch up.

Which of the Italian city-states' institutions facilitated such an unexpected economic flourishing? Of the most important was the *corporation*, an institution born with a very general meaning of association among non-family partners who shared common goals and governed themselves. The university – the earliest in Bologna in 1088 – was a corporation of professors and students who were free to teach and learn; the monastery or convent was a corporation of monks or nuns, who shared a specific mission and a specific brand of religiosity within the Catholic church; the chamber of merchants was a corporation of merchants who developed their own rules and also administered justice in the case of disputes; the guilds were corporations of specific manufacturing trades, and so on. Being democratically self-governed on the basis of statutes drafted by its members, the corporation acted in the common interest of its members, who were in the best position to develop the most appropriate rules, including establishing common standards and apprenticeships. It is only many centuries later that corporations became outdated institutions incapable of keeping up with the need for innovation and as such were abolished. However, the business corporation retains to this very day the older meaning of an organization uniting people who work for a common goal. The municipal government had the role of balancing the power of the various corporations and of ensuring public goods (including education) – a role that was not easily exercised and which gave rise to conflicts, but for many centuries was successfully maintained. Since the fourteenth

Table 1.1 Per capita GDP (in 1990 dollars) in some European countries, 1000–1850

	1000*	1300	1400	1500	1570	1650	1750	1850
England/Britain	757	742	1099	1058	1111	925	1695	2774
Low countries	760	876	1195	1454	1432	2691	1874	2355
Northern-Central Italy	450	1620	1751	1533	1459	1398	1511	1481
Spain	500	864	819	846	910	687	583	1079
Portugal	450	na	na	600	na	na	1248	923
Germany	400	na	na	1146	na	948	1050	1428
France*	470	na	na	727	na	860	na	1597

Source: Bolt and van Zanden, *The First Update to the Maddison Project: Re-estimating Growth Before 1820,* Maddison Project Working paper 4, 2013.

Notes: * From Maddison's original database, www.ggdc.net/maddison

century, governance became increasingly concentrated in the hands of the "signoria", strong men and their descendants capable of maintaining law and order.

Entrepreneurs able to develop their businesses inside the corporations showed great creativity in establishing economic institutions suited to growth. The following lists some of the most important ones, which have left a permanent mark on the evolution of the world economic system:

1. The *commenda* (also known in Venice as *collegantia*). The twelfth century saw the development, primarily in the maritime cities, of a form of business based on capital advanced by people without family ties and which was managed by business agents. Those who provided capital ran the risk of losing only that portion employed in the business (limited liability). This was the first form of the joint-stock company.

2. *Insurance*. The first steps towards building up insurance funds were taken in the twelfth century in the maritime republic of Venice to address the high risks taken by ship-owners who carried goods by sea. Insurance significantly lowered their business risk.

3. *The bank*. Lending practices existed everywhere, but the banks created in the Italian medieval cities were linked to merchants' activities. The banking practices that were developed – such as letters of credit or currency exchange – enabled credit flows to finance commerce over vast areas. As credit allowed merchants to invest in increasing jobs for citizens, the Catholic Church slowly abandoned condemning usury for such practices as credit for productive purposes, making them morally acceptable. Credit to consumers, instead, was made available through special institutions with donated capital – the *Monti di Pietà* (pawn banks) – that were the earliest form of "microcredit". Public banks also emerged, originally specializing in loans to states – "public debt" – in order to, for example, support a war,

provide famine relief, or finance public infrastructure. These public banks were the earliest form of central banks.

4. *Double-entry accounting.* This way of comparing revenues with expenditures was already known in the Islamic world, but was perfected by Italian merchants, beginning with Leonardo Fibonacci in Pisa in 1202. The Franciscan monk, Luca Pacioli, mathematician and economist, who also collaborated with Leonardo da Vinci, theorized this approach in 1494 in a dedicated treatise.

The necessity of recording an ever-increasing number of contracts also led to the emergence of a new profession, the public notary, who played the role of guarantor of the legitimacy of a transaction concluded in his presence, which took on the value of a public act. At the University of Bologna a special curriculum was developed to prepare these new professionals.

The wealth generated in the Italian city-states through their innovative approach to business enabled the birth of the Renaissance. Beginning in the fourteenth century a vast cultural movement originated in Italy and spread throughout Europe encompassing literature, art, music, education, philosophy, science, politics, religion, fashion and the way of living, greatly assisted on the one side by the invention of printing (of German origin in 1454, but immediately adopted in Italy), and on the other by the diffusion of patronage among the rich merchants and aristocrats as well as the Catholic clergy. Patronage facilitated the decoration of churches, palaces, public buildings, squares, gardens, hospitals and also the creation of cultural centres, libraries, academies and theatres. Patronage together with the demand for furnishings for private palaces created a market for high quality durable goods. Urban planning developed, with the opening up of larger and straighter streets covered in stone, the building of additional squares, and infrastructure such as the provision of clean water and sewage.

The number of artists, architects, philosophers, intellectuals, musicians, poets and writers who lived in Italy during this period remains a source of wonder and one can mention here only a few of the most famous figures. Among the writers, poets and philosophers, the triad of Dante (Alighieri) (1265–1321), Francesco Petrarch (1304–74) and Giovanni Boccaccio (1313–75), all active in Florence, stand out as figures who promoted humanism, gave dignity to the Italian language and shaped modern poetry and literature. *The Divine Comedy*, Dante's first major literary work in Italian, is still today studied in all Italian high schools. In architecture, Filippo Brunelleschi (1377–1446), creator of the dome of Santa Maria del Fiore in Florence, is widely considered to be the first modern architect and engineer. Other architects, painters and writers of treatises were Leon Battista Alberti (1404–72), active in Rome, Florence, Rimini, Ferrara, Mantua, and Donato di Angelo Pascuccio, known as Bramante (1444–1514), active in Milan and Rome. But perhaps the three most important artists were Raphael (1483–1520), primarily a painter, but also active in planning the reconstruction of St Peter's Basilica in Rome; Michelangelo (1475–1564), who also played a major part in its building and painting, as well as in the decoration of many other churches; and Domenico Fontana (1543–1607), the most famous architect of his time. The Republic of Venice too had its own artists, including the architect Andrea Palladio (1508–80); the painters Piero della Francesca (1416–92), Andrea Mantegna (1431–1506), Paolo Veronese (1528–88), Giorgione (1478–1510), Tiziano (1490–1576) and Tintoretto (1519–94). And of course there was Leonardo da Vinci (1452–1519). Alongside his paintings of huge technical originality were his innumerable contributions to the fields of astronomy, anatomy, botany and engineering, which included hydraulics, fortifications, solar energy, bicycles, cannons and machines for flight. In this list of Italian geniuses we must also mention Niccolò Machiavelli (1469–1527), philosopher, writer, statesman (he was secretary of state of the Republic of Florence between 1498–1510, in the brief time when the Medici family was not in power), known for his major work of political philosophy, *The Prince*.

This artistic and scientific flourishing of Italy cannot be understood without noting both the level of economic advancement of the Italian city-states, which provided the resources needed to pay for the work of those engaged in the planning and construction of buildings and churches, and that competition was extended from the economic field to the fields of culture and art. Italian cities competed not only in trade and banking, but in attracting and supporting the best artists, artisans and scientists, who were appointed as professors in universities and masters of the construction and decoration works, allowing them to form their own schools. This attracted foreign students, who attended Italian universities, art and music schools, giving rise to the "grand tour" phenomenon, which could last up to several years and which took in all the important northern and central cities of the country. The attraction of Italian artists and thinkers to those abroad ensured the spread of Renaissance culture, art and ideas and new economic practices across Europe.

DECLINE AND *RISORGIMENTO*

Such prosperity, which had not only produced the highest level of urbanization in the world, but had changed the agriculture of the country as well, was not going to last. Between the end of the sixteenth century and the first half of the seventeenth century, Italian manufacturing and trade contracted, the woollen industry and shipbuilding were almost entirely lost and the Mediterranean Sea fell under the control of northern European navies (Dutch and English). If the Italian standard of living did not fall proportionately (see Table 1.1), it was only because the Black Death had reduced the Italian population by 20 per cent in the first half of the seventeenth century. The situation did then improve, but it was followed by another fall in economic activity in the second half of the eighteenth century, such that the Italian standard of living was eclipsed first by the Dutch and later by the British in the eighteenth century (neither Germany nor France were significantly ahead of Italy in the middle of the nineteenth century and Portugal and Spain still remained behind).

This surprising decline has prompted much research to establish its causes. While the geographical explorations of the sixteenth century, which opened up trade routes in the Atlantic and the Pacific, moved a large amount of trade away from the Mediterranean, this does not explain the unwillingness of the Italian sea republics to engage in Atlantic trade, or the loss of the continental European markets formerly supplied by the Italian city-states. Most explanations point to institutional rigidities. Corporations continued to practice their trade as they had done successfully up until then, without taking into account the rise of markets for lower-cost manufacturing that necessitated less skilled workforces and lower wages. Italian wages were also kept high by an agricultural sector that could not accommodate higher consumption standards (there are simply not enough plains in Italy) and which increased the price of foodstuffs. The efforts by the city-states to defend their freedom from other city-states ended ultimately in no longer being able to prevent the larger newly built European states from invading areas of the country and imposing their rule, in the midst of continuous wars, famines and epidemics. In a nutshell, the Italian city-states ceased to creatively solve the problems produced by the advances they had initiated. However, relative decline did not entail a fall into backwardness and malaise, but rather a loss of leadership. The grand tour continued for a long time, as did developments in the arts and sciences, up until the Enlightenment, to which Italy offered important contributions.

In the field of art, Rome became the home of another cultural movement – the Baroque – which spread across Italy and Europe, reaching its finest incarnation in Spain. Famous architects, such as Gian Lorenzo Bernini (1598–1680), Francesco Borromini (1599–1667) and Luigi Vanvitelli (1700–73), continued to build churches and palaces. Rome owes to Bernini the grandiose square facing St Peter's. Caserta owes to Vanvitelli its famous royal palace. The sculptor Antonio Canova (1757–1822) spearheaded neoclassicism and the architect Giuseppe Piermarini (1734–1808) is celebrated for his theatres, among which is Milan's *Alla Scala*. Although the tradition of performing theatrical pieces with music dates back to the Renaissance, these years witnessed the work of such dramatists as Pietro Metastasio (1698–1782), who wrote texts complemented with music by Gian Battista Pergolesi (1710–36), Alessandro Scarlatti (1685–1757) and many others, leading up to the creation of full operas by Gioacchino Rossini (1792–1868). Among the world renowned painters we can cite Michelangelo Merisi, known as Caravaggio (1571–1610), Giambattista Tiepolo (1696–1770), Giovanni Barbieri, known as Guercino (1591–1666), Guido Reni (1575–1642) and the three Carracci, mostly active in Bologna.

Galileo Galilei (1564–1642) is best known for his clash with the Catholic Church over his denial of the Ptolemaic conception of the universe, but as a physicist, mathematician, philosopher and astronomer, he produced hugely original work to back Copernicus's intuitions. Other early scientists worthy of mention are Lazzaro Spallanzani (1729–99), who made contributions to the fields of zoology, botany and physiology; Marcello Malpighi (1628–94), known especially for his studies of the lungs; Luigi Galvani (1737–98), who made important advancements in bioelectromagnetics (the process of "galvanization" comes from his name); and Alessandro Volta (1745–1827), who built the first electricity generator. All taught in Italy's best universities alongside the thinkers who paved the way to the Italian Enlightenment of the late eighteenth century. Both its southern (Naples) and northern (Milan) branches made major contributions to the development of the European tradition of civil rights. With his book *Dei delitti e delle pene* (1764) Cesare Beccaria (1738–94), of the Milanese school, was the first to argue against the death penalty, as well as being a significant economist. Antonio Genovesi (1713–69), perhaps the Neapolitan school's most famous representative held in Naples the first university chair in the world officially denominated for "commerce and mechanics" for which he wrote his lectures on "civil economy". The Italian Enlightenment schools cultivated an economic theory that shared much with that of the Scottish Enlightenment (more than with the French), but had a more pronounced orientation towards "public happiness", namely a fair distribution of the fruits of economic and technical advancement among the population through the help of good government supportive of the "common good".

The Napoleonic governments, which lasted for a short time in various parts of Italy, provided an opportunity to introduce some economic reforms inspired by Enlightenment ideas. Following the defeat of Napoleonic France, at the Congress of Vienna in 1815, Italy was divided into seven states (see Figure 1.1). The republic of Genoa, which had remained independent until the Napoleonic invasion, was merged with the Kingdom of Sardinia under the control of the Savoy family, who had originally governed a duchy encompassing Piedmont and Savoy before adding the island of Sardinia in 1720. The Kingdom of Sardinia was the only Italian state that had managed to remain independent from foreign powers. The remaining northern area comprised the Lombardy–Venetia kingdom, under the direct control of the Austrian emperor. Lombardy had fallen under Austrian control in 1714 (after almost two centuries of Spanish rule) and it had enjoyed the fruits of an enlightened governance, especially during the years of Maria Theresa's rule. Venetia, instead, had remained independent as a republic until the Napoleonic invasion. The Vienna Congress brought Lombardy together with Venetia to form the Lombardy–Venetia kingdom. In the northern part, there were also the two small duchies of Parma and Piacenza and of Modena and Reggio, the former was put under the governance of the second wife of Napoleon Marie-Louise (who was Austrian), and the latter governed by the local aristocratic family D'Este, which had marriage ties to the Hapsburg family. The central part of the country comprised the Grand-Duchy of Tuscany, formerly independent, but governed by a member of the Austrian imperial family (the enlightened Leopold II) and the papal states (which also included the Northern provinces of Bologna and the Romagna). In the south, the Kingdom of the Two Sicilies was the largest Italian state, already unified in the twelfth century first by the French and then by the Spanish, with a branch of the Bourbon family becoming established as monarchs there and governing after the Vienna Congress under the protectorate of the Hapsburg empire.

The realization that only the unification of the country and the recovery of self-government (this time as a nation state) could rescue Italy from stagnation resulted in the *Risorgimento*, a process which was to take more than four decades. It was led by a small number of reformist intellectuals across the country, who, capitalizing on international events, sought to

Figure 1.1 Map of Italy after the Congress of Vienna, 1815

Source: Wikimedia Commons/Enok

rally the people to protest and revolt. It was only in the 1840s, especially in the revolutionary year of 1848, that less authoritarian ruling governments were finally established with the granting of constitutions in the Kingdom of the Two Sicilies, in Tuscany and in the Kingdom of Sardinia. The southern king withdrew the constitution after only five months, but Carlo Alberto, Sardinia's king was persuaded to lead the independence movement, waging war against the Hapsburg empire to "liberate" the country from Hapsburg rule. The war lasted for more than a year, but was lost and Alberto abdicated. His son Vittorio Emanuele II however did not withdraw the constitution and instead started to put in place the conditions for a second attempt at liberation. The Kingdom of Sardinia became host to all the expatriates from Italy's other states (that had returned to their former authoritarian governments), and became the home of the *Risorgimento* movement. Vittorio Emanuele II found in Cavour a prime minister able to promote economic advancement as well as arrange the necessary diplomatic alliances.

Camillo Benso, Count of Cavour (1810–61), had in the 1840s written several economic essays while active as an entrepreneur in creating new joint-stock companies in industry and infrastructure. He had supported the introduction of the constitution and had been elected as a member of the first parliament. After the defeat and abdication of Carlo Alberto, he was selected by the new king first as minister of agriculture and commerce, then as minister of finances, and then as prime minister in 1852. He modernized the state apparatus and financial system, instigated the building of railways and other infrastructure, created joint-stock banks, and patched up a crucially important alliance with France.

The second war of independence against the Hapsburgs, waged in 1859 with French support, was a success. It however only gained the territory of Lombardy. The annexation (the cost of which was to hand over Savoy to France) however was followed by several uprisings across the centre-north of the country, which prompted the annexation in 1860 of the two small duchies of the Po Valley, the Grand Duchy of Tuscany and the entire papal states, excepting Rome and its surrounding area. The southern kingdom was added in 1861, as a result of a daring and unanticipated campaign led by the adventurer Giuseppe Garibaldi, who was able with just a few soldiers to spark the revolt of the local population and defeat the Bourbon army. The new Kingdom of Italy was proclaimed on the 17 March 1861, Venice was added in 1866 after a third war, and finally, Rome after a campaign against the pope in 1870, which was accomplished without any fighting. Trento and Trieste were only added after the First World War.

So it was that a small kingdom like the one governed by the Savoy family proved capable of unifying Italy, not through the power of its army, but through the shrewdness of a man like Cavour, the widespread participation of Italian intellectuals – including the writer and poet, Alessandro Manzoni (1785–1873) and the opera composer, Giuseppe Verdi (1813–1901) – as well as adventurers like Garibaldi, and the wider population, who were aware and proud of the Italian traditions of self-government.

LIBERAL ITALY AND FASCISM

Cavour died of malaria a few months after the proclamation of the Kingdom of Italy, but there was no shortage of learned and capable men to build on the legislative foundations he put in place in the Kingdom of Sardinia.[1] New legislation making elementary education compulsory and free for boys and girls was enacted in 1859. The introduction of income tax in 1864, a measure at the time only seen in Britain, created a harmonious fiscal system that allowed stability and sustainability for a century, placing public debt under control. Following the British model, the new kingdom adopted the gold standard and free trade, but this latter decision proved too hasty (as Italian industry did not take off), and a mild form of protectionism for specific sectors (cotton textiles, paper, ceramics, sugar, steel) was reintroduced in the period, 1878–87. Protection of cereals was also introduced to avoid a precipitous exodus of farmers from the countryside. Italy experienced some difficulties in maintaining the gold standard for the entire period up to the First World War, but remained with it most of the time.

The decision to put in place a central bank, however, was delayed for decades. Italy had too many banks of issue inherited from its previous states (in Tuscany alone there were two), and none wanted to give up their prerogatives. It was only when a banking crisis developed at the end of the 1880s and a number of banks, including some banks of issue, were on the verge of bankruptcy that the government was able to create the Bank of Italy, which began its operations in 1894. Although this did not prevent the failure of some of the existing banks, it allowed the reconstitution of new joint-stock banks, inspired by the new German model of mixed (or universal) banks, which acted as both deposit and investment banks, and which allowed the cultivation of strong relationships with the industrial enterprises they supported through their loans.

This new body of legislation did not receive a uniform reception across the country, because the various regions that had been unified did not share similar economic conditions, or similar civic traditions. In particular, the north–south divide that characterizes Italy to this very day was already established, although more apparent in the social and cultural background of the population than in the actual standard of living, which did not vary much given the lack of industry everywhere. The former Kingdom of the Two Sicilies (henceforth "the South") was the only part of the country that saw popular revolts against the new state. More people died in these revolts (sometimes labelled as a "civil war"), which were supressed by the army, than in the wars of independence. These revolts were typically led, not by soldiers belonging to the defeated Bourbon army, but by outlaws and bandits, so called brigands (this episode in Italian history is known as "brigandage"),[2] able to take advantage of the poor communications (roads in the South were inadequate) and the lack of control over the territory by the central authorities. The new government was prepared to enforce the rule of law over the entire territory and at the peak of the conflicts (1863–5) the Italian government was forced to deploy half of the entire Italian army in the South.

The southern population had many reasons of its own why it was unable to rid itself of the brigands: Italian civic traditions were lacking in the

South because, as already mentioned, city-states were unable to develop there and protracted Spanish rule had not allowed local governments to introduce effective measures for economic development. Infrastructure was insufficient, trade diversification modest, banking unpromoted and agriculture eclipsed all other sectors. Perhaps the worst shortcoming was that at unification, almost 90 per cent of the population of the South were illiterate, while in all other areas of Italy the situation was better and in some regions much better.[3]

It is no surprise, therefore, that when industrial take-off finally materialized in the years 1880–1914, most of it was located in the north-west of the country, in the three regions of Piedmont, Liguria and Lombardy, forming an "industrial triangle" joining up the regions' three capital cities, Turin-Genoa-Milan. Some ten million people – about a third of the population – lived in the industrial triangle, yet it was home to some two thirds of the country's industrial activity, as was demonstrated by the first Italian industrial census of 1911. Modern industries were established: cotton textiles, steel, transport (bicycles, motorbikes, automobiles and planes), electricity (particularly hydroelectricity, because of the lack of coal) and chemicals. Italy's poor natural resources meant that raw materials had to be imported. Only the traditional production of silk (both raw and manufactured), which had survived from the past, initially ensured enough exports, together with some special agricultural produce, to support imports. Despite the small territorial basis of its industrial take-off, the country started to catch up with other advanced European nations.

The First World War brought a premature end to this process and had a devastating effect on the country (in spite of it having been on the winning side) not only in terms of loss of life (700,000 soldiers lost their lives and around 600,000 civilian casualties, mostly as a result of epidemics), but in terms of the dislocation of state finances and the disruption and disorganization of its prior political development. Public debt (mostly loans from the United States and Britain) rose to a fantastic peak; bankruptcies were widespread, social unrest became violent and the liberal political system was shattered. This context gave rise to a new political movement led by the former socialist, Benito Mussolini, and which took its name of *fascist* from the Roman symbol of the fasces (bunches of ears of wheat). In the aftermath of war, Mussolini was able to take advantage of the many weaknesses of the country, present himself as a guarantor of law and order, and persuade the king, Vittorio Emanuele III, to appoint him as prime minister after his "march on Rome", carried out by a few thousand ill-armed supporters, on 28 October 1922. The army, which did not take part in the march on Rome, could certainly have been used to restore order, but the king decided differently. By the end of 1925, Mussolini had turned his government into a dictatorship.

Mussolini sought to solve the problems of public finance. Firstly, following the enactment of the *Bonifica Integrale* (Integral Land Reclamation) law in 1923, he instigated a long-term process of investment to tackle the poor infrastructure of Italian agriculture. Secondly, in 1926, Giuseppe Volpi, the minister of finances, successfully negotiated the cancellation of Italy's foreign debt with the United States and Britain, relieving the public finances of the financial burden of the war. And thirdly, the financier Alberto Beneduce, called in by Mussolini to help with the rescue of the Italian banking and industrial system after the 1929 crisis, created in November 1931 a new type of investment bank with public capital. The Istituto Mobiliare Italiano (IMI) raised funds to finance business by selling bonds to the public with state guarantees and was destined to replace the mixed banks that were in trouble. After the Second World War this became the model for other banks, which were responsible for financing Italy's reconstruction and economic miracle (see Chapter 2). In January 1933, Beneduce introduced a public holding company, the Istituto per la Ricostruzione Industriale (IRI), for the industrial corporations that the state had bailed out. Hugely powerful, it owned around 20 per cent of the stocks of all Italian joint-stock companies and controlled some 40 per cent of them. It included the entire arms industry, 90 per cent of shipbuilding, 80 per cent of shipping companies, all of the country's air transport industry, all the telephone companies and the radio business, 40 per cent of the steel industry, a third of the engineering sector, the former mixed banks that had been reduced to deposit banks, plus smaller percentages of other industrial sectors. Legally, however, the IRI was not nationalization, because IRI companies retained their private incorporation and were administered independently of national bureaucracy.

Fascism did not interrupt the industrialization of Italy, but it had two major effects. Firstly, it placed under state control a vast array of banks and industrial companies, a legacy that the Italian republic was to leave in place for a long time after the Second World War. Secondly, it did nothing to counteract the serious falling behind of the South. Before the First World War, the liberal governments had started to introduce specific measures of support for the southern economy, but such efforts were curtailed by war and the need to finance the production of arms, located in the industrial triangle. After the end of the First World War, public spending was again mostly directed to the North, in order to avoid major bankruptcies. Similarly, Beneduce's bail-out along with the modest effort to produce armaments during the Second World War, concentrated public spending again in the North. It is true that the regional disparity in the economy had existed before the First World War, but in the interwar period it was only to worsen.

Although Mussolini enjoyed significant public support after he rose to power, the loss of public support came when he allied with Hitler in the late 1930s, began the persecution of Jewish communities, something that many Italians did not approve of, and embarked on war without adequate preparation. Widespread organizations of *resistenza* against both fascism and the German occupation grew up across the country and fascism was overthrown on 25 July 1943. Mussolini was imprisoned but, rescued by Hitler, he gained control of the North under German occupation, as the Allied armies landed in the South. On 25 April 1945 Italy was fully liberated and Mussolini was killed by the *resistenza* three days later, while trying to escape to Switzerland. A new life started for Italy.

2

The Italian economic story, 1946–2016

Fascism was a dictatorial regime that left its negative mark on the country's culture, society and legislation, but it did not interrupt the process of industrialization, which was resumed immediately after the restoration of democracy, although the general conditions of Italy and the rest of Europe at the end of the Second World War were dismal. This chapter charts the evolution of the Italian economy in the period 1946–2016. I have broken down the period into five phases:

1. *Reconstruction* (1946–51). The birth of the republic and the integration of Italy within the international economy; administration of the Marshall Plan;
2. *The economic miracle* (1952–73). A period of rapid modernization;
3. *The return of instability* (1974–92). Economic growth continues, albeit more slowly; a period of political gridlock and the accumulation of a large amount of public debt; niche firms prosper;
4. *Incomplete reforms* (1993–2007). Continuing political turmoil and persistent high public debt levels; participation in the Eurozone places Italy on an slow and volatile economic path, despite the many reforms enacted and the resilience of Italian industry;

5. *Italy and the global economic crisis* (2008–16). One of the worst performers during the world financial crisis.

This chapter will familiarize the reader with the key events, both domestic and international, that have affected the Italian economy, while Chapters 3–5 will focus in detail on the macroeconomic, microeconomic and social analyses, providing quantitative illustrations.

RECONSTRUCTION, 1946–51

Major political and institutional changes took place in Italy immediately after the Second World War. A referendum was held on 2 June 1946 on whether to retain the monarchy, which had not supported democracy in Italy, or to introduce a republic. Support for a republic prevailed, however with a narrow margin of only 54 per cent of the votes. And for the first time women could exercise their right to vote, which had been acquired by decree during the war. The transition from monarchy to republic was peaceful and on 13 June the king left for Portugal. On the same day the referendum was held, Italians voted for 556 representatives of the newly created Constitutional Assembly, which, over 18 months, drafted the new constitution that came into force on 1 January 1948. On 28 April 1948 there was the first election of the new republic. Previous governments had been temporary, based on the parties that had supported the resistance to fascism. Some were a reconfiguration of parties that had previously been abolished by fascism – the Partito Socialista Italiano (PSI), the Partito Comunista Italiano (PCI) and the Partito Liberale Italiano (PLI) – but one was a new creation – Democrazia Cristiana (DC) – which was formed in 1942 by former members of the Partito Popolare Italiano (PPI) and was led by Alcide De Gasperi (1881–1954).

De Gasperi is one of the most praised politicians of post-Second World War Italy. Born near Trento when the region still belonged to the Hapsburg empire, he was elected in 1911 to the Austrian parliament, representing the Italian province of Trento. With the Italian victory in the First World War and the amalgamation of the province with Italy, he became a member of the new PPI and was elected to the Italian parliament. After the closure of parliament by Mussolini, he was arrested and imprisoned. Released under pressure from the Catholic hierarchy, he was exiled in the Vatican state (recognized by Mussolini in 1929) as an employee of the Vatican library. In 1942, he was instrumental in the creation of the new Catholic party, Democrazia Cristiana, and in December 1945 he was appointed prime minister by the king and continued in this role under the republic, first leading national coalitions of all parties and between May 1947 and August 1953 forming governments with the support of the centre parties. It was De Gasperi who led DC to its brilliant victory in the 1948 elections (achieving 48% of the votes) and who strengthened Italy's position within the West, benefitting considerably from the Marshall Plan.

The first two years after the end of the war were spent in appeasing the country and preventing retaliations,[1] in coping with food shortages and the need for housing, in repairing infrastructure and plant, and in re-establishing relations with the United States and the rest of Europe. When it became clear that the US was to launch a major plan for reconstruction in Europe, the Italian government sought to put inflation and credit under control, stabilizing foreign exchange. On the fiscal side, although interventions were delayed until 1951 (with the reform known under the name of the DC politician who drafted it, Ezio Vanoni), the situation was stable, because public debt had been cut to very low levels by the war and immediate postwar inflation. Between the summer of 1947 and the summer of 1948, with the new constitution in place and with full democratic government rule, it was possible to shape the plan for growth required by the Marshall Plan and so benefit from the distribution of resources coming from America.

The vision of the government was to use such external resources to increase the capacity of basic industry (steel, electricity, oil, chemicals, engineering) and to rebuild and modernize its infrastructure.[2] This meant high levels of investment for industry and infrastructure to the detriment of social expenditure. Given the widespread misery and the lack of employment at the time, it was a courageous approach, one that did not even gain a consensus amongst the Americans, who feared a possible rise of support for the communist and socialist parties from an impoverished population. De Gasperi was able to persuade the US that he was in full control of the domestic political situation, and the plan went ahead, accompanied by the adoption of some structural projects that intervened in the social field. In addition, in order to speed up decision-making and to utilize an existing body of well-trained managers, IRI, the public holding company put in place by fascism, was left in place with a new statute, and the public investment bank IMI was selected as the bank to administer the Marshall Plan funds earmarked for investment.

Most of the investment plans for basic industry were conceived and implemented inside IRI,[3] which acted through a number of existing sectorial sub-holdings, including Finsider (Società Finanziaria Siderurgica) for steel, STET (Società Finanziaria Telefonica) for telephones, Finmare (Finmare Società Marittima Finanziaria) for shipping companies, and in 1948, Finmeccanica[4] for engineering industries. The republic had inherited from fascism two state-owned oil and gas companies: Azienda Generale Italiana Petroli (Agip) and Società Nazionale Metanodotti (Snam). Enrico Mattei, an entrepreneur who had been active in the *resistenza*, was given the mandate to privatize them, but argued that the development of the oil and gas industry was of strategic importance and instead recommended the continuation of state control. Later, he would persuade the government to build another state holding, Ente Nazionale Idrocarburi (ENI), founded in 1953, by bringing together Agip, Snam and other companies. ENI under Mattei's presidency became a major protagonist of the subsequent economic miracle.

Of special importance was the IRI plan for steel, prepared by the engineer Oscar Sinigaglia, who pushed the government to join the European Coal and Steel Community (ECSC), the first step towards European integration. Italian steel plants were small and limited, but Sinigaglia and others understood that for the Italian engineering industry to grow it needed a much larger steel capacity and the Marshall Plan could offer the initial resources to build it. When the ECSC came about in the early 1950s, Italy was ready and keen to participate and this allowed the country to collaborate, as a founding member, in the subsequent steps of European economic integration.[5]

Relations with the United States during the Marshall Plan years were successful in promoting a modernization of Italian industry not only by introducing economies of scale and assembly line production processes, but also in business organization and marketing, which prompted changes in university curricula in business administration. These relations also allowed for a reconfigutation of Italian trade unionism. The social democratic and Catholic components of the trade union confederation, Confederazione Generale Italiana del Lavoro (Cgil), increasingly in disagreement with the violent protests of their socialist-communist brothers, decided to form their own unions. The Catholic constituency formed the Confederazione Italiana Sindacati Lavoratori (Cisl), which derived inspiration from the American model of trade unionism, while the social democratic unionists and others belonging to the small centre parties formed the Unione Italiana Lavoratori (UIL), a much smaller organization than the other two. This configuration of Italian trade unionism has remained in place to this very day, with the addition of smallish independent unions.

In social policy, the De Gasperi governments implemented three key initiatives. In 1950–51 the dismantling of *latifundia* was achieved. In several parts of Italy, particularly in the South, large landed estates had survived, which were not only inefficiently managed but which were worked by peasants under particularly miserable conditions. Through expropriations, 700,000 hectares of land were redistributed to landless peasants who were helped to transform these estates into more productive cultivations. The second key policy initiative was the launch in 1949 of a vast programme of house building, aimed both at replacing the houses destroyed by the war and upgrading the existing stock of inadequate housing. A parliamentary inquiry on "misery" at the time showed that at the beginning of the 1950s only half of all apartments had running water and an inside toilet, with the situation much worse in the countryside.[6]

The third, and most ambitious, initiative, was the resumption of a policy that had been discontinued during the First World War and not reactivated since, namely a set of measures specifically addressed to promoting the southern economy. The association, Sviluppo Mezzogiorno (Svimez) was set up in 1946 to study ways of encouraging growth in the South, which had seen itself fall further behind the rest of the country in the interwar years. The work of the association and its lobby led to the creation, in 1951, of Cassa per il Mezzogiorno ("Fund for the South", often abbreviated to "Casmez") an agency specifically aimed at stimulating economic growth in the South. In its first years, Casmez concentrated on investing in the improvement of agriculture, but towards the end of the 1950s it had begun supporting programmes of industrialization. The agency remained in place until 1984, when it was replaced by another smaller agency up until 1992. The workings of Casmez did not entirely solve the "southern problem", but, together with emigration abroad (which the De Gasperi governments strongly encouraged) and internal migration from the South to the North, the situation was relieved, indeed the South saw its per capita income grow slightly more than in the North until the early 1970s (see Chapter 3).

In conclusion, during the reconstruction period the Italian governments did not miss any of the important opportunities offered to it by the settlement of the Second World War: participating in all international organizations that were created; working effectively with the United States; investing massively for the promotion of industry; facing up to the most urgent social problems; and stabilizing monetary and fiscal policies within the gold standard. After the creation of the International Monetary Fund and the general round of adjustments in exchange rates that it prompted – in order to make the gold exchange standard sustainable – Italy did not devalue the lira until the demise of the fixed exchange rate system in 1973. For these reasons De Gasperi and the DC of those times have had the respect of most commentators.

ECONOMIC MIRACLE, 1952–73

Reconstruction paved the way to Italy's "economic miracle", a period of sustained high growth rates, among the highest in Europe, lasting to the beginning of the 1970s (curbed only by a brief inflationary surge in 1963–4). Italy's growth model of "structural change" was one adopted by other European countries. Investments in industry and in infrastructure continued unabated, so that much of the underemployment in agriculture (44% of the labour force in the 1951 census) was absorbed into more productive activities in manufacturing, transport and other services. The tourist industry was revived and came to play once again a supporting role in keeping the balance of payments balanced, as it had done before the First World War. Within industry the period marked a great switch from textiles and general light industry to metal engineering and chemicals (see Chapter 3).

The technical and organizational models imported were American ones, adapted to the much smaller size of Italian companies (a topic that will be discussed in Chapter 4). Exports grew at a rate double that of GDP, thanks certainly to the lower cost of labour, but also to the creativity of Italian entrepreneurs and the formation of the customs union (Common European Market) agreed in 1957 in Rome by the same six countries of the ECSC. Despite the strategic role played by exports, it cannot be maintained that this was export-led growth – exports were only 10 per cent of GDP in 1951, and only reached 14 per cent in 1971. It was domestic demand that was driving the economic miracle. Increasing income levels fuelled the demand for the products of the second industrial revolution, namely cars, household appliances, pharmaceuticals and a great variety of new plastic goods like telephones and televisions. In 1951 there were around 425,000 private cars on the road; in 1971 it had reached 10 million. Regular television broadcasts began in 1954 with only 88,000 subscribers; by 1971, 82 per cent of Italian families had a television (and 86% a refrigerator and 63% a washing machine). Modernization of the distributive sector also followed American lines, with the introduction

29

of supermarkets, although it was a process delayed by legislation and it was not until the reforms of 1971 that distribution structures were fully liberalized.

Geographically, all parts of the country contributed to the national economic miracle, including the South supported by Casmez. The new and defining feature of this period of growth was the take-off of the north-east of the country, followed at some distance by the centre, with its unique development of specialized small and medium-sized enterprises (SMEs) in fashion, engineering, building materials, furniture and hundreds of niche products, from spectacles to jewellery, from musical instruments to buttons. These SMEs often bunched together in areas that became known as "industrial districts", specialized in one single type of product in all its variety. These SMEs proved capable of exporting and of sparking a catch up with the historically powerful industrial triangle (see Chapter 4). At the time of writing, the centre of the country remains at some marginal distance behind the North-East (see Chapter 3).

This phenomenon has given rise to the notion of "Three Italies", a term first coined by Arnaldo Bagnasco (1977)[7]: the original centre of development in the North-West (the industrial triangle), hosting the largest of the Italian corporations; the South, which never developed a spontaneous form of industry; and the North-East–Centre, which developed in the 1960s/1970s on the basis of its SMEs. The "Three Italies" approach has been adopted ever since as it remains the best way to summarize the differentiation of the Italian economy.

To strengthen the local dimensions of the Italian state, in 1970 legislation was enacted that instituted the "regions" as separate political entities, and which applied to the constitution a more decentralized articulation of the governance of the country. At unification, centralization à la Français was the preferred model, because of the fear that the historic divisions of the country would never be overcome. But, after many decades of centralized government, the new constitution sought to nurture the advantages of decentralization. It took more than 20 years, however, before the regions were actually put into place, initially only with administrative functions.

It was only with the reform of Part V of the constitution in 2001 that the legislative power of the regions was fully strengthened.

This flourishing of the Italian economy (which will receive a more precise statistical analysis in Chapter 3) was engineered by countless new entrepreneurs, who complemented established big businesses like Fiat (cars), Montecatini (chemicals), and Italcementi (cement) as well as state-owned holdings. ENI became an innovative oil company, launching joint-ventures with companies of oil-producing countries, including an agreement with the Soviet Union for the import of oil and branching out into petrochemicals. Its brilliant chairman Enrico Mattei lost his life on 27 October 1962 in an air accident, when his private plane exploded. Efforts to establish whether it was an assassination have continued to this very day, without any firm conclusion. Mattei left a company so well organized that it continued to prosper, becoming one of the largest oil companies of the world.

IRI was also active, entering new business areas, like television (through its radio company); motorway construction with its new sub-holding company Autostrade (1950); airlines, with Alitalia (1957); ship-building, with Fincantieri (1959); and the food and beverages industry. At the peak of its life in 1980, IRI could boast 557,000 employees and was active in a range of key industries. IRI (and also ENI) worked in combination with Casmez to develop industry in the South, diverting many of the investments of their companies to southern regions, in particular to petrochemical and steel plants, but also for car, aircraft and train manufacturing. There is a vast literature on the impact that these initiatives had in the South. Many support the view that these produced "cathedrals in the desert", mostly capital intensive plants, the intermediate products of which were often shipped to northern Italy to be transformed into finished goods. There is little doubt, however, that this was the most coherent and sustained effort to industrialize the South, with partial, but not negligible results.

In 1962, another public holding company was created, EFIM which brought together engineering companies that had fallen under the control of the state. A better solution would have been to merge them into Finmeccanica, which had already shown able to reorganize its companies, but for reasons connected with Italy's spoils system, this solution was not adopted. Of all Italy's public holding corporations, EFIM was the worst managed and in 1992 it was liquidated, only then passing most of its companies to Finmeccanica. If we put together all the state-owned holdings and the largely public financial sector, one can argue that the economic miracle was hugely supported by an Italian state directly engaged in strengthening the supply side of the Italian economy by means of a vast programme of investments in infrastructure and basic industry.

If Italy's economic miracle was for the most part achieved through the imitation of industrial technology already in existence, there were a few sectors in which Italy was innovative.[8] Perhaps the most interesting one was the invention of plastics (technically, isotactic polypropylene) in 1954 by Giulio Natta, who would go on to receive the Nobel prize for chemistry in 1963. Italy took full advantage of Natta's invention with the company Montecatini, which had financed his work together with the Milan Polytechnic and became one of the world's largest producers of that polymer, forming the basis for several different categories of products, given its endless adaptability. Another field for innovation was nuclear technology. Indeed, the Nobel prize-winner Enrico Fermi, who built the world's first nuclear reactor in the United States in 1942, was an Italian expatriate. In 1952 a national research centre on nuclear technology was established and the first European nuclear reactor was opened in northern Italy in 1959, becoming the basis for Euratom, the European Atomic Energy Community. In 1963 the largest European nuclear power plant was opened in central Italy, followed by others. By the end of the 1960s Italy hosted one third of all European nuclear capacity and collaborated at the European level in all the research projects in this field, a leadership lost in the 1970s and finally buried by a referendum in 1987, which put an end to the construction of nuclear plants in Italy.

There are two other advanced fields in which Italy was innovating: space and electronics. Italy was part of the European team for space research, which gave rise to the European Space Research Organization in 1962, and also created its own research centre in 1963, where the San Marco programme was developed. In 1964, Italy was the third country in the world (after USSR and US) to launch a satellite with an American carrier, maintaining its presence in the field of satellites and aerospace to this very day. The aerospace centre Telespazio was opened in 1963 (the fourth centre of that type in the world), and still manages space infrastructure today. In electronics, Italy excelled in the development of radar and missiles, with the foundation of companies that are still thriving today inside Finmeccanica (renamed Leonardo in 2016). Within a different application of electronics, the company Olivetti, which manufactured typewriters, created in 1959 *Elea 2003*, one of the first computers with transistors, although it was unable to build on this invention, which was later sold to General Electric. The Italian government understood the opportunities that these innovations could open up to the country and approved new legislation that earmarked public funds in support of applied research, but this innovative line of enterprise was lost in the crises of the 1970s and 1980s.

Little new happened, by contrast, in banking and the shape of the sector remained the one inherited from the 1930s. Italy maintained a bank-based system, where a large amount of capital for investment came from the banks (and not from the stock exchange, which remained small). This differed to the German bank-based system of universal banks (banks which performed both the role of investment bank and deposit bank) since by the 1930s Italy had moved to a separation of long-term and short-term credit functions. Long-term credit became fully state-owned, through the establishment of "special credit institutes", of which the first, IMI was founded in 1931. The limited capital of these banks was assembled from state-owned or non-profit banks, and they financed investments through the issuing of bonds, which enjoyed state guarantee and had therefore a low level of risk. Many more of these banks came into existence after the Second World War, the most well known of which was Mediobanca (1946). Mediobanca was created by the three banks (Banca Commerciale

Italiana, Credito Italiano and Banco di Roma) that had fallen under the control of IRI when bailed out by Beneduce. Unhappy at having their operations diminished, they formed a "special credit institute" controlled by them, so that they could indirectly continue to operate long-term investments. The new bank was placed in the hands of Enrico Cuccia, an experienced banker, who was CEO of Mediobanca until 1982. Under the direction of Cuccia, Mediobanca became the Italian investment bank most closely connected with international finance and most dedicated to strengthening private entrepreneurship, while IMI was mostly (although not wholly) connected with state-owned or state-promoted industry.

Short-term credit was granted by savings banks (which were non-profit), state-owned banks, banks owned by IRI (as a result of the bail out operation mentioned in Chapter 1), credit unions, and popular banks (themselves cooperatives, although under different legislation). Only a modest slice of short-term credit (20%) was in the hands of fully pri-vate banks, generally of small size. Although there was sufficient finance available in Italy, the system was highly fragmented and the widespread use of state-guaranteed bonds to finance investments placed all the risk on the shoulders of the state. As long as the economy did well, problems were limited, but, as we shall see later, when the world became much more unstable, the need for banking reform became pressing.

Italy started the period with 44 per cent of its labour force still employed (or perhaps more precisely, underemployed) in agriculture, producing 24 per cent of GDP. Twenty years later 20 per cent of the labour force was still working in the primary sector, producing 9 per cent of GDP. In those twenty years, 5 million farmers moved to other jobs often in other parts of the country or emigrated abroad. The exodus out of agriculture was to continue, with a further 3 million farmers leaving. Today less than one million workers are left in the primary sector, 4 per cent of the labour force. Improvements in the efficiency of Italian agriculture proceeded slowly after the abolition of latifundia, also because the Common Agri-cultural Policy (CAP) introduced by the European Union in 1962 did not initially cover typical Mediterranean products, many of which were not included until the 1980s. Today, Italian agriculture has increased its production of typically Italian raw materials for the food and drinks industry: horticulture, grapes, olives, citrus fruits, pigs (for ham), milk (for cheeses), local brands of cereals and more.

Emigration and internal migration were two emerging phenomena, which declined dramatically in the 1970s. Between 1946 and 1970 net migration abroad was 3.1 million people (gross emigration was 6.7 million), with approximately half going to those European countries in need of unskilled labour (Switzerland, Germany, France, Belgium) and half going outside Europe. Most emigrants came from the South, but other areas (such as Venetia) contributed as well. The bulk of Italian emigration to the United States had already taken place between the 1880s and the 1940s, but the exodus was so large that over the entire period from unification to 1985, migrants to the US (and Canada) accounted for almost a third of the total of around 19 million Italian emigrants.

Internal migrations of people leaving the countryside to move to cities that were rapidly industrializing or offering new jobs in services and in public bureaucracy increased steeply. Rome increased its population by 1 million between 1951 and 1971, Milan and Turin added half a million each, but most cities enlarged, involving millions of new inhabitants, without building up enormous megacities. At the peak of the movement, between 1958 and 1963, 1.3 million southerners left for the industrial cities of the North; between 1955 and 1974, the South lost 2.3 million people to the centre-north region.[9] Turin became a third "southern" city (after Naples and Palermo), as a result of the influx of immigrants from the South arriving on so-called "sun-trains". The problem of housing became explosive, and temporary slums were unavoidable. Popular housing schemes progressively solved it, although not always in the best way, leaving some peripheral districts, especially of Rome and Naples, with poor urban planning.

At the level of macroeconomic policy, governments were led by the DC, which kept monetary and fiscal policies under control; inflation was generally low, public finances showed modest deficits and exchange rates remained easily fixed at the 1949 level (625 lire per dollar). The focus of Italian governments was mostly concentrated on the administration of policies on the supply side of the economy, rather than on the demand side: control of state-owned companies, projects to be developed in the South with Casmez, popular housing programmes, planning (see below) and participation in the process of European integration. Italy was a signatory to the treaty establishing a customs union, Euratom, the European Investment Bank (EIB) in 1957 as well as CAP in 1962.

The DC, unable to master an absolute majority in parliament until the beginning of the 1960s, formed coalitions with smallish centre parties, but 1962 saw a famous (in Italian history!) "*svolta*" (shift, or turnaround) when the DC embarked on an alliance with the socialist party, PSI. The PSI after the war had been a faithful ally of the communist party, PCI, but during the 1950s it became increasingly dissatisfied with being associated with unpalatable Soviet policies and was ready to cooperate with the DC, provided the DC would be supportive of more "leftist" policies. In 1962 agreement was reached between PSI and DC leaders on a range of fundamental issues: nationalization of the private electricity companies, accused of running local monopolies; controls over speculation in urban real estate; and tighter state planning of the economy, following the French example.

This "*svolta*" did not prove unproblematic and both the PSI and the DC lost votes in the 1963 elections. At one end was a constituency of the DC who did not approve of the alliance and at the other end was a splinter group from the PSI which advocated even more leftist policies. The resulting new centre-left government was formed by DC leader, Aldo Moro, who saw no alternative. It was an alliance that was to prove long-lived, but chiefly because of the many disruptive events that followed. However, from the point of view of the macroeconomic policies adopted, only the nationalization of electricity was accomplished, with the creation of the state-owned company ENEL in 1963, and there was an increase in the compulsory school age to 14, which raised the level of education of the country. The rest of the programme remained in progress for a few years, not helped by an explosion of inflation in 1963–64 that required a restrictive monetary policy in order to avoid having to leave the gold exchange standard. This meant a curbing of growth rates for two years, followed by a resumption of growth more concentrated on exports, but it was the events of 1968–69 that were to profoundly shake the already weak political equilibrium. Widespread protests began in the universities in 1968 followed by large-scale strikes by workers in 1969, an episode known as the *autunno caldo* ("hot autumn")

The latter part of Italy's economic miracle was achieved within an international context that had lost the stability of the earlier years. The United States was engaged in a wearing war in Vietnam that produced inflation and protests at home; Mao Zedong, in China had launched the "cultural revolution", raising hopes that there could be an alternative path to communism to that of the Soviet Union, which in 1968 had violently repressed Dubcek's "velvet revolution" in Prague. University students in the United States and Paris first, and then in many other European countries, protested for a more open and peaceful society. In Italy this movement was strong and sparked a liberalization of university admission criteria, granting the freedom to choose any curriculum regardless of the type of high school attended. It also paved the way to a new culture of permissiveness that led to the introduction of divorce (1970), to a profound change in family law recognizing equal rights for women (1975), and to the right of abortion (1978).

The mobilization of workers for higher pay, better working conditions and more employment rights was even more disruptive and affected many countries, including Belgium, Sweden, Britain and even Germany. In Italy, after an increasing number of strikes throughout 1968 and 1969, it reached its peak between September and December 1969. There were many reasons on the part of Italian workers to be unhappy: the increase in wages had not kept pace with the economic miracle, hours of work were too long, workers had no rights to be informed or consulted on matters concerning changes of management in their workplaces, the welfare state was less than universal and not adequately organized, although many subsidies had been granted haphazardly. Some of the protests became violent and some of the trade union representatives began speaking of revolutionary prospects. To heat up a situation that was already quite dangerous, on 12 December 1969 inside a bank located near the centre of Milan a bomb exploded killing 16 people. It marked the beginning of a period of bombings perpetrated by various right-wing groups.[10]

Employers and the government were in a difficult position, and in December 1969 new contracts more favourable to workers were signed by employers' organizations, while the government drafted a new bill on workers' rights – the so-called "workers' statute" – which was approved by parliament in May 1970. This law has always been considered the "flag" of the Italian leftist parties, because it drastically restricted the freedom to dismiss workers on the part of employers. Article 18 of the law stipulated that a dismissed worker could appeal to a court and, if the court recognized his/her case as valid, they had to be reinstated in their job. The law also prohibited all types of control on the working activity of employees by third parties or mechanical instruments; it also prohibited ideological discrimination of workers (in appointments and in lay-offs) and allowed more freedom in the organization of trade union activities in the working place. An important provision of the law was that it was applicable only to plants or offices that employed more than 15 workers. There is general agreement that this provision has discouraged the enlargement of Italian firms.

But the impact of the "hot autumn" went further than the workers' statute. It inaugurated a period of great tension between workers and employers, which was further exacerbated by a radicalization of some leftist students and workers into political-military structures that were to organize kidnappings and assassinations. These groups, of which the Red Brigades (*Brigate Rosse*) was the most significant, first appeared in 1970, but until 1973 their actions were limited to bombing buildings. The *Anni di piombo* ("years of lead") will be discussed in the next section as they directly relate to the period 1974–92. What is useful to note here is that precisely when the Italian economic miracle had to give way to a consolidation of a newly born or greatly transformed Italian industry, two disruptive events took place: domestic terrorism and international instability. The demise of the gold exchange standard and the rise in the price of raw materials (mainly oil) turned terms of trade negative for Italy and opened up deficits in its balance of payments. How industrial corporations and Italian governments reacted to this new much less favourable context is the subject of the next section.

RETURN OF INSTABILITY, 1974–92

The return of global economic instability was the result of three main factors: the demise of the gold exchange standard between 1971 and 1973; the organization of a cartel of oil-producing countries (OPEC), which in 1973 agreed to raise (treble) oil prices; and the international political tensions created by the Vietnam war, which culminated in the withdrawal of US troops from Saigon in 1975. The general tendency to manage the economic consequences of all of these disturbances through inflation did not help because it only further added to the instability.

Italy faced this return of instability at the very moment it had to face substantial increases in the cost of labour and at the same time that it had to reorganize its welfare system. In this latter regard, several measures were introduced, including the improvement of maternity leave and the introduction of unemployment subsidies (1968–72), the relaunch of popular housing (1972), and the implementation of a universal national health service (1978). The government sought to meet these larger welfare expenditures through increased taxation, but the 1974 bill that approved this (the so-called "Visentini law") proved immediately insufficient, while growth rates of GDP plummeted and the Italian balance of payments turned negative because of Italy's dependence on oil imports.

These difficulties were multiplied by the activities of the Red Brigades, which threatened Italian democracy.[11] Originating in 1970, their use of violence began with bombings of industrial plant and the property of employers and right-wing political figures, but escalated to attacks on individuals in 1972–73 when employers were kidnapped and later released. The first killings began in 1974 followed by an escalation of attacks, despite the police making an increasing number of arrests. Managers, industrialists, intellectuals, journalists, judges, prison guards, policemen, politicians, trade-union leaders and many others were killed or wounded. The height of the attacks was reached with the kidnapping of the politician Aldo Moro on 16 March 1978.

Moro, who had engineered the agreement between the DC and the PSI in 1962 (see above) was working to form a political alliance even with Italy's communist party, in order to tackle the serious difficulties Italy faced during the economic and political emergencies of the mid 1970s. He sought to cut off any possible external support for the Red Brigades from some of the PCI's more revolutionary wings;[12] to strengthen the resolve of the Italian PCI to distance itself from the Soviet Union; and to rally the entire country together to face the terrible challenges of the day. Moro was ready to lead a government of "national solidarity" with PCI representatives, but what actually came to pass in 1976 (after the widespread success of the leftist parties in the elections) was a DC government led by Giulio Andreotti with the external support of PCI votes. In 1977, revolutionary unrest again reached the universities and a number of intellectuals, not only Italians, rallied to support protesters against police repression.

Moro was kidnapped because the Red Brigades saw in his political efforts the end of their chances of launching a revolution. The 55 days Aldo Moro was held captive was probably the worst challenge faced by the Italian Republic (or First Republic, as it is called today). The government obviously could not accept the conditions for Moro's release, and was unsuccessful in finding where he was held. The Red Brigades, throughout his captivity, released letters and statements drafted by Moro, which held the attention of the entire country. Even the pope got involved, offering himself in place of Moro. It has never been clarified whether Moro could have been rescued, but the fact is that he was killed on 9 May. The 63 people involved in his kidnapping were later captured, convicted and sentenced: 26 of them receiving life sentences and the others receiving

a total of 1,800 years in prison. The cruelty of this episode and its reper-
cussions marked the beginning of the defeat of the Red Brigades and other
violent groups.

Kidnappings and killings did not end immediately, but the awareness
spread that the moment for revolution had passed and a number of the
revolutionary groups began to lose members, while arrests multiplied as
police became better organized and some of the arrested Red Brigades
members became informers. The years 1979–81 were still bloody years,
but by 1982 killings had become exceptional events. There was an effort
to rebuild some of the groups in the late 1990s, which saw the murder of
two professors instrumental in drafting labour market reforms (Massimo
D'Antona in 1999 and Marco Biagi in 2002). Over the whole period around
100 people were killed by the revolutionary groups, who were formed of
some 500 active members, with an estimated 5,000 external supporters.

In the face of these domestic and international challenges the government's favoured policy instrument appeared to be a highly accommodat-
ing monetary policy, that produced increasing rates of inflation. Adding to
this spiralling inflation was the 1975 pact between the trade unions and the
Confederation of Industrialists led by the patron of Fiat, Gianni Agnelli.
In the midst of the Red Brigades attacks and the many "wild cat strikes",
Agnelli agreed to the request by trade unionists to protect wages against
inflation according to a principle of "wages as the independent variable".
A *scala mobile* (sliding scale) was agreed that would automatically adjust
wages to inflation every three months, which in turn critically contributed
to speeding up inflation throughout the subsequent price adjustment.[13]
From a rate of 11 per cent in 1973, inflation reached its peak at 21 per cent
in 1980.

Towards the end of the highly troubled 1970s, a decision taken at the
European level had an important impact on the Italian economy. The
demise of the Bretton Woods system of fixed exchange rates resulted in
a great divergence in the monetary policies of the EU members, which
threatened the continuation of the process of economic integration. To
rescue it, several projects were discussed for rebuilding monetary stability

inside the EU and in March 1979 the European Monetary System (EMS) was instigated, a system of fixed but adjustable exchange rates. It was politically unacceptable for Italy not to participate, even though its rates of inflation were the highest among EU members. To contain the number of adjustments needed by the Italian lira to participate in the EMS, the decision was taken to change position on monetary policy, which enabled a disinflationary trend. To strengthen and guarantee this trend, in the summer of 1981, the treasury minister (the economics professor Nino Andreatta) devised a so-called "divorce" between the treasury and the Bank of Italy, which was no longer obliged to buy all the treasury bonds not absorbed by the market. The Bank of Italy, therefore, had the means to counteract inflation, which indeed was reduced to 6 per cent by 1986 and continued to decrease subsequently.

The Bank of Italy also had to face a series of banking scandals, which cost the resignation of the governor of the bank, Paolo Baffi in 1979, and the killing in the same year of the liquidator of one of the banks under scrutiny (Banca Privata Italiana), Giorgio Ambrosoli.[14] Problems continued with another bank (Banco Ambrosiano), the CEO of which (Roberto Calvi) escaped abroad and was later found hanged in 1982 under Blackfriars bridge in London. By the mid-1980s, the banking system was back to normal. In part because the ultra right masonic organization "P2", led by Licio Gelli, which had been implicated in the collapse of Banco Ambrosiano and other financial crimes, was outlawed in 1982, as a result of a parliamentary commission of enquiry led by the DC's Tina Anselmi.

It is in this context that one of the most significant events for the future of the Italian economy took place. Rather than realizing that fiscal policies also needed to work to contain the state deficit, governments oversaw a move in the other direction. State budget deficits, which had run at around 10 per cent in the 1970s, but which had not converted much into increasing public debt because of the high inflation, were to reach an average of 12–13 per cent per year: so it was that in the presence of pronounced monetary disinflation, public debt rocketed to 105 per cent in 1992. We shall see later the dramatic impact that this had in 1992 and in subsequent years. Here I shall explain the reasons for such an imbalance. The chief reason was the political deadlock in which the country had plunged in the 1980s. The "historical compromise" between the DC and PCI did not survive the death of the two leaders who had conceived it: Aldo Moro was killed and Enrico Berlinguer, secretary of the PCI, died in 1984 of a stroke. In addition the PSI saw the ascent of a strong leader, Bettino Craxi, (prime minister between 1983 and 1986), who sought to move his party towards the centre ground of Italian politics, while seeking to diminish the DC's historical role. While working towards this end, he did not refrain from using funds acquired through corrupt practices.

Indeed, the level of corruption in Italy had increased enormously. Other parties (the DC especially) sought to protect themselves from loss of power by the same means. Along with corrupt practices, the electoral use of public finances was enhanced: the years of Craxi's premiership were those with the highest state budget deficits, despite not being poor from an economic point of view. The watershed came in 1992, when a pool of Milanese judges (among whom the most famous was Antonio Di Pietro) made several arrests of prominent industrial and political figures on charges of corruption, among them Craxi himself, who in 1994 escaped to his villa in Tunisia, where he was to live for the remainder of his life.

The initiative of the Milanese pool of investigators, known as *Mani Pulite* ("Clean Hands") had far-reaching impact, initiating a crisis within all the existing political parties and a series of suicides of important businessmen involved in corruption. At the 1994 elections, which were run under a new electoral law, the Left won 34 per cent of the votes, with the leading party being a new iteration of the PCI;[15] the Right 43 per cent, with the major party being Forza Italia (FI), a newly formed party created by Silvio Berlusconi, a media tycoon. What remained of the DC had formed a new party, the Partito Popolare (PP), the old name of the Catholic party, that together with other smallish centre parties received only 16 per cent of the votes. Ever since, Italian politics has tried to find a new modus operandi but instability remains its key feature.

While Italian politics was deteriorating in the 1980s, big business was also struggling. Trade union militancy, Red Brigades attacks, inflationary tendencies and anti-corporate legislation were not conducive to the health of major firms, perhaps best illustrated by the fate of the Italian chemical firm, Montedison. Italy had inherited from the past a substantial chemical company, Montecatini, which had become even larger when it merged with another company in the 1960s to form Montedison. Ill-conceived legislative decisions, which allowed other smallish chemical companies to enlarge through public funds without having the conditions to become competitive, coupled with the efforts of the chemical branch of the state-owned ENI to gain control of Montedison, were not conducive to the survival of the company, which was broken up and sold in the 1990s, destroying a once-great Italian chemical company.[16]

Other large companies, similarly, did not prosper, as we shall see later in the chapter. Of the state-owned enterprises (SOEs), only ENI did well. Enel and IRI both got in trouble because the government decided not to raise tariffs on public services, not to lay-off workers, and to enlarge their plants in the South, all decisions that produced large budget deficits and prevented innovative investment. Not all SOEs suffered in the same way, but certainly they lost the opportunity to strengthen. The introduction in Italy in 1990 of anti-trust legislation was only undertaken because it was required by anti-trust legislation introduced in Europe, and certainly not because it was needed by Italy's industrial structure, which hosted very few large companies, most of which were under state control.

While big business experienced difficulties, SMEs flourished and their exports were able to support the balance of payments in a surprising way. However, over the long run, the success of Italy's SMEs has created a problem that the country is still grappling with today. Public opinion, including a number of influential economists, became convinced that "small is beautiful" and that a country like Italy could do without big business. Italian culture has always had an affinity with small business dating back to its medieval artisans. The goal of *"mettersi in proprio"* (starting one's own business) remains the dream of every Italian citizen, who would prefer not to work for a boss, unless this boss is a family member, friend or partner. It was therefore too easy for Italians to buy into this idea, and disregard the truth that globalization works against small business. We shall see in the next section that a new development in industry, in the 1990s and the first years of the twenty-first century, was to improve the situation, although the problem remains largely unresolved.

In 1992, all these weaknesses – of political and economic instability – resulted in a major blow. The world's financial markets, having been liberalized in 1990, saw Italy as the weak country inside the EMS, and in the summer of 1992, international speculators started to attack the lira, bringing Italy to the verge of an insolvency crisis. A new government was formed in July 1992 led by an independent PSI member (and law professor), Giuliano Amato, which immediately introduced strong measures to reverse state budget deficits, including, without warning and imposed in a single night, a tax of 6 per 1,000 on all bank deposits. This was enough to stop the crisis, but not to prevent Italy's exit from the EMS in September. Amato in the few months in which he was prime minister also enacted a bill for the privatization of all Italian SOEs and a reform of the Italian banking system, again in the direction of privatization. He marked a significant break with the past and a watershed for the Italian economy, which since then has searched for a new equilibrium, albeit one difficult to find.

INCOMPLETE REFORMS, 1993–2007

After 1992, the Italian economy became a construction site for continual reforms, always urgent, but never completed. Against a background of increasing world economic instability (even Germany was in difficulty[17]), Italy faced the challenges of participating in the next phase of European integration – a common currency, the euro – which had been discussed in the late 1980s and approved, with an Italian signature, at Maastricht in February 1992. Of the convergence criteria that the EU members had to meet, Italy met none: inflation and interest rates were higher than the average, state budget deficits and public debt were distant from those required and Italy was no longer in the EMS (it was a requirement of the transition period both to be inside the EMS and not to have devalued currency in the previous two years).

As we have seen, a few months after the signature of the Maastricht treaty Italy was thrown out of the EMS, and the whole process of becoming part of the new project seemed under jeopardy. At that point Italy faced a choice: either to give up and remain outside the euro (as Britain, Sweden and Denmark had done, all for different reasons), or radically change its approach to public finances. Italy chose the second course and embarked on a never-ending effort to get public finances under control. We should note that these attempts involved primarily an increase in taxation rather than cuts in public spending as a number of fiscal reforms were unsuccessful in curbing expenditure.

Notable success was achieved in pension reform. In 1992, the Amato government raised the retirement age from 60 to 65 for men and from 55 to 60 for women. It also remained possible to retire, at an earlier age, with 35 years of social contributions. In 1995, the decision was taken to move, in the future, from a defined benefit (DB, PAYGO) system to a defined contribution (DC) system. Since then, pensions have been continuously reformed, raising the retirement age (currently 66 for both men and women) and cutting benefits, while early retirement still remains an option with 42 years of contributions. Voluntary schemes have also been promoted. Although state pension funds are now in equilibrium, no cap has ever been imposed, so today the Italian welfare system remains overburdened with pensions payments, made more acute by an ageing population, as we shall see in Chapter 3 when we examine the Italian welfare system in more detail. At this point we can say that successive governments have lacked the courage to reshape the welfare system – developed on the basis of successive additions and subtractions – to make it more coherent and effective.

As we've seen, this was a period of volatility in Italian politics. After 1994 Italy saw change of governments between the Right and the Left, something not seen before the demise of the Soviet Union. The key to understanding the instability of Italian politics following the demise of the historical parties is that governments were based on coalitions, usually between a large party and smaller allied parties. These smaller parties could leave at any time, creating the need to form a new government or bringing about new elections. The elections of 1994 were a case in point: won by the centre-right led by Berlusconi, within a few months the government had collapsed as one of their allies had parted company. After a few months of "technocratic" governments, new elections in 1996 brought the centre-left, led by Romano Prodi[18], to government, followed by Massimo D'Alema in 1998, who had to relaunch the centre-left government with a partially new composition, after a small coalition partner broke away. In the 2001 elections Berlusconi won again and governed until 2006[19] – an unusually long term of government. When in new elections Romano Prodi came back, his coalition had too narrow a margin of votes in parliament and his government failed, in 2008, again because a small party in his coalition withdrew support.

Prodi's centre-left government took the decision to join the euro in 1996, and the Maastricht convergence criteria were met by 1998, with the exception of public debt, which having been accumulated over a long period, could not be straightened out in such a short span of time. Italy promised to cut the debt with the proceeds of state privatizations, something that indeed had started happening. Of the state-owned holdings, IRI was dismantled in 2000 and its sub-holdings privatized, although not all entirely; Efim had been liquidated in 1992, ENEL and ENI were privatized (although the state still owns a substantial share; see Chapter 4); banks too were largely privatized, with several mergers, notably producing two big banks, Unicredit and Intesa-San Paolo, but still leaving many smaller ones (see Chapter 4). When the process came to a conclusion around 2005, the shrinking of public debt had plateaued, but Italy was still some way from the 60 per cent target of public debt to GDP.

Other reforms were carried out, but often without a long-term vision. If pension reforms, although not entirely satisfactory, had met their targets of putting public expenditure under control, the large decentralization of the Italian administrative system into regions worked in the opposite direction. After the decision in 1970 to implement regional autonomy, progress in doing so was slow. The first major step forward was only taken in 1997–98, with the implementation of laws delegating many central functions and duties to local authorities, followed in 2001 by the first major reform of the 1948 Italian constitution, which granted the regions administrative control of all those functions that did not require a national level of administration alongside substantial legislative powers. Only a few branches of public administration – foreign policy, immigration, defence, monetary policy, the design of the welfare state – were left with the central authorities. This constitutional reform certainly afforded opportunities for the regions to shape their own policies and to be more responsible to the needs of their local communities, but it could not prevent less responsible regions from spending too much and being bailed out by the state. In addition, duplications and unnecessary expenditures were multiplied, especially on the many matters in which regions and the central state had coresponsibility.

Both education and the labour market were also the subject of reforms. In the field of education, no comprehensive reform had been introduced since the reform of the early 1960s that extended compulsory schooling to 14 years of age. In 2000 a new law (the Berlinguer reform) was approved, which added two additional years to basic schooling and reshaped the existing curricula. Since then, it seems that all new governments have wanted to add something in this area and in 2003 (the Moratti reform) and in 2010 (the Gelmini reform) centre-right governments have approved other laws aimed at connecting education with the needs of the labour market. These repeated changes to education legislation have not helped teaching staff to commit to long-term projects, especially when so many of them had temporary contracts. This has produced a school system which is far from satisfactory (see Chapter 5).

Concerning the labour market, Italy followed the EU trend of introducing more flexibility in the labour market, with the 2003 Biagi reforms (named after the labour law academic Marco Biagi who had drafted it and who was murdered by the Red Brigades). Legislation made possible multiple types of new employment contract, all of them temporary, which made jobs for young people much more precarious than ever before, while not altering existing legislation concerning those who had a permanent job. The consensus among economists is that, in a context like the Italian one of small-sized enterprises, this new labour market legislation allowed the survival of many weak firms, making the Italian economy more vulnerable to the world crisis that followed.[20]

Concerning the South, Casmez remained in existence until 1984, being replaced by a smaller agency (AgenSud) until 1992. Since then, governments have relied on EU structural funds intermediated by the Italian regions, but there has not been any coherent policy to replace the kind of structural interventions devised by Casmez. As we shall see in the following chapters, the position of the South in respect to the rest of the country has been frozen, with some regions doing slightly better than others, but on the whole with no capacity to continue to close the gap as had been done in the years of the economic miracle. Southern regions have not, in general, been up to the challenge of developing projects that could really have an impact on changing their economic structures, instead they have ended up using either EU or Italian funds ineffectively or only for clientelistic redistribution. To their partial justification, one could say that it was only after the constitutional reform of 2001 that they could really function with more autonomy, precisely when the world problems had multiplied, as we shall see in the following section. It remains one of Italy's major unsolved problems, not least because the lack of development in the South has strengthened criminal organizations, which remain endemic there (see Chapter 6).

In the midst of such turmoil, the rate of growth of the Italian economy plummeted. For the first time since the Second World War, Italy was growing at a slower pace than the rest of Europe. To support what little growth remained, a new industrial phenomenon developed, that has become known as "fourth capitalism".[21] This fourth capitalism emerged out of the industrial districts, when some firms started consolidating amongst themselves, including buying similar firms or establishing plants abroad, to become highly specialized "pocket multinationals". In this way, these firms, mostly of intermediate size, became capable of internationalizing (not just exporting), of controlling foreign markets directly, and being able to innovate as a result of their larger size. Today Italian "niche capitalism" is made up of these firms, which we shall examine in Chapter 4.

THE WORLD ECONOMIC CRISIS, 2008–16

The 2008 global financial crisis hit Italy harder than the 1929 crisis, an exception among advanced nations. The reasons are easily found: smaller firms were not equipped to face such a major fall in demand, especially in the domestic market, while the already high public debt and European requirements to stabilize the euro prevented the Italian governments from any expansionary public spending. In addition, the inherent instability of Italian politics, which has already been outlined, was a further component to the weak reaction of the Italian economy.

After the fall of the second Prodi government in 2008, early elections followed, in which Berlusconi won for a third time. This last Berlusconi government proved utterly inadequate to face the crisis, and in November 2011, in the midst of a financial storm that had pushed Italy to the verge of insolvency, it was substituted by a technocratic government led by the university professor Mario Monti, who had served as a European commissioner in charge of competition and anti-trust policy, with the mandate to carry out important reforms. In the 2013 elections, the centre-left won, but again by a very narrow margin, squeezed in part by the success of Movimento 5 Stelle (M5S), the Five Star Movement, a new party created in 2009 by Beppe Grillo (a popular comedian) and Gianroberto Casaleggio (the head of an IT company), with the aim of renewing political representation, by means of an alleged web democracy and the presentation of candidates without previous political experience. Its programme cut across left and right, blurring established lines and produced in Italy a three-party system, something mirrored in other European countries (but typically with ultra right populist parties in place of M5S).

The formation of a new government proved extremely difficult as M5S was not ready to enter into coalition, but after long negotiations it was finally led by Enrico Letta, who charged for being too slow in promoting reforms, was soon substituted by Matteo Renzi, who instead worked hard to bring about reforms, albeit not always with success. Perhaps the most important was the so-called "Jobs Act" (2014), which sought to relax the rigidity of permanent jobs by abolishing "article 18" of the workers' statute of 1970 (which imposed on employers the return to work of workers laid off, should a court find in their favour). It also sought to benefit permanent jobs, by discharging employers from part of their social contribution payments, while diminishing the types of temporary contract and making them more costly. The Jobs Act was fought by the leftist trade union CGIL, which is still trying to have it abolished.

Reforms in public administration have sought to cut waste and high remunerations. In education, efforts have been made to address the temporary status of hundreds of thousands of teachers; although there remains a backlog, the situation is normalizing. New legislation to stimulate growth and social entrepreneurship in the third sector has also been accomplished. In the field of human rights, civil unions were made legal and divorce was made easier. In addition, there have been measures to increase the income of the lower classes, which had worsened during the crisis, through the distribution of benefits and the abolition of a number of taxes, although these measures have been widely criticized because they have been introduced outside of an overall framework for the revision of the welfare state. And in 2017 the long expected reform of the machinery of justice (generally considered too slow and ineffective) was approved.

Matteo Renzi engaged most of parliament's time, however, with a new constitutional reform which sought to make the approval of new legislation much simpler, by turning the senate into a house of the regions, with a hundred members elected in regional elections. This reform was accom panied by a new electoral law for the chamber of deputies, which granted a majority premium to the largest party, provided that it won 40 per cent of the votes. Renzi succeeded in having both measures approved by parliament, but the former was rejected by referendum in December 2016, after which Renzi resigned, and the latter was reinterpreted by the constitutional court. At the time of writing, a new electoral law has been finally approved, with a third of seats elected by a majority system and the rest with a proportional one. After the resignation of Renzi, another government was formed, led by Paolo Gentiloni, which continued the reformist stance of the Renzi government up to the March 2018 elections, which saw the M5S win 33 per cent of votes and the coalition of centre-right parties win 37 per cent, while the left party PD achieved only 18 per cent. At the time of writing (June 2018) a new government was formed between the M5S and one of the parties of the centre-right coalition, namely the Lega, based on a "contract" seeking to bring together some of the basic goals of the two parties, which had won the elections on widely different programs.

Although the Italian economy has revived since 2014, it proceeds at a very slow pace, because investments are still lagging behind and public debt is not shrinking. In addition, Italy has suffered in recent years from major natural disasters including two large earthquakes, the first in 2012 in Emilia Romagna and the second in 2016 in central Italy. Indeed, in 2012, Italy ranked third in the world's list of countries hit by natural disasters. In 2014, the arrival of thousands of migrants mostly from Libya, only added to Italy's problems. In that year, the number of asylum seekers arriving in Italy reached 170,000. After a small drop in 2015, the number increased to 181,000 in 2016, with most of them coming from unstable sub-Saharan African countries. The costs of these flows are high, not only from hosting these migrants, but also in rescuing them from the sea, a very demanding activity carried out with great engagement and professionality by Italian ships in collaboration with others.

At the time of writing none of these problems have been solved, but 2017 did see a substantial acceleration of economic growth, which is giving the country some hope for the future. Also, the migration issue has finally been addressed and some amelioration has been achieved, namely a decrease in flows. However, as in many other European countries, the country is now divided between those who believe the solutions to Italy's difficulties can better be found if Italy leaves the European Union, or at least from the single currency, and those (the majority at the time of writing) who instead believe that it is time to strengthen Italy's European ties in a renewed pact for growth and collaboration. Italy has been a not insignificant part of Europe for 3,000 years, with ups and downs, and there is no reason to think that it will withdraw from Europe, but it remains to be seen whether Italy will remain in Europe as a weak and marginal partner or as a strong and active one.

3

Measuring the Italian economy

We are now in a position to illustrate quantitatively the evolution of the Italian economy over the period 1945–2016. Typically, it is not an easy exercise to piece together over a long period data published by national statistical offices (in Italy Istat, founded in 1926 by the statistician Corrado Gini). These data are constructed to produce short-term comparisons and, as a result of international agreements, the methods of construction of aggregates often change, making it difficult to compile long-run series. Fortunately, as part of the celebrations in 2011 of the one hundred and fiftieth anniversary of a unified Italy, both Istat and the historical office of the Bank of Italy have collected and homogenized existing historical series, precisely for the purpose of building up a coherent long-run analysis. In particular, the historical office of the Bank of Italy, which had already began to revise Italian GDP historical series at the time of its hundredth anniversary in 1993, decided to complete the task by producing a renewed and highly sophisticated 1861–2013 GDP series.[1] In this chapter I will examine five key macroeconomic aspects of the Italian economy: 1) population and employment; 2) GDP, productivity and the movement of prices; 3) the foreign sector: exports, imports and the balance of payments; 4) the public sector: the budget, public debt and the welfare state; and 5) monetary policies. A final section will be devoted to institutions, which have only recently undergone measurement.

To keep the chapter manageable, I have not detailed in the tables each single year, but only those years marking watersheds or in need of specific explanations. The regional breakdown of the series is presented when relevant, using North-West (NW), including Piedmont, Liguria and Lombardy; North-East (NE), including Venetia, Friuli, Trentino-Alto Adige, Emilia-Romagna; Centre (C), including Tuscany, Marche, Umbria, Latium; and South (S), including all the remaining regions. International comparisons are used chiefly to highlight the current situation of Italy. An examination of the detailed features of the productive structure of the Italian economy is deferred to Chapter 4, while Chapters 5 and 6 will provide an analysis of two strategic dimensions: the human factor and the social factor. Here, in this chapter, one can find the aggregate picture.

POPULATION AND EMPLOYMENT

Table 3.1 shows the key characteristics of population for the census years, and this will also be the point of reference for most of the other tables. It can be seen that there was a natural increase in population due to fertility rates exceeding two children per woman (column 6) until the end of the 1970s; thereafter fertility rates dropped below the replacement rate (approx. 2.1) and population continued to increase only as a result of immigration (column 7), particularly significant since the late 1990s.[2] For long a country characterized by emigration, with very few of its population born abroad, this immigration has dramatically reversed the trend (which we shall discuss further in Chapter 5). The regional distribution of population across the "Three Italies" has not changed markedly over time (columns 2–4), but in the years following the 2008 world crisis the South has lost population, as a result of high unemployment. Life expectancy has substantially increased and Italy now has one of the highest percentage of its population over 65 in the world, the implications of which in terms of welfare shall be spelled out later.

Table 3.2 presents rates of employment and shows that activity rates

Table 3.1 Population: life expectancy, fertility, migration, 1951–2011

	Resident population thousand	NW %	NEC %	S %	Life expectancy years	Fertility rates %	out-/in+ migration rate %
	1	2	3	4	5	6	7
1951	47,516	24.7	38.1	37.2	65	2.3	-2.8
1961	50,624	26.0	37.3	36.7	69	2.4	-2.8
1971	54,137	27.6	37.5	34.9	72	2.4	-3.1
1981	56,557	27.0	37.5	35.5	75	1.6	-0.5
1991	56,788	25.9	36.9	35.6	77	1.3	2.2
2001	56,996	26.2	37.8	36.0	80	1.3	6.1
2011	59,434	26.5	38.8	34.7	81	1.3	4.1

Source: Istat, census data

Table 3.2 Employment and unemployment, 1951–2011

| | Total (thousands) | of which unemployed | rate of unemployment % | activity rates on pop 15–64 | | |
	1	2	3	Total 4	M 5	F 6
1951	20,279	1,500	7.4	66.0	90.1*	29.4*
1961	20,760	1,108	5.3	62.3	82.6*	27.3*
1971	19,586	1,100	5.6	56.8	85.1	31.2
1981	21,098	1,623	7.7	58.0	78.1	40.3
1991	23,073	2,039	8.8	59.5	75.8	44.7
2001	23,473	2,164	9.2	61.5	74.6	50.1
2011	24,789	2,057	8.3	63.4	72.8	51.4

Note: *on population 10–64; activity rate is the amount of people employed and those unemployed actively searching for a job as a percentage of the total population.

Source: labour force comes from the reconstruction in C. Giordano, F. Zollino, 2015, the remaining data are my elaborations from Istat.

in Italy have never been high. Historically this has been because of a very low rate of female participation in the labour force. Until the 1970s, Italy was not alone in this, but whereas in other advanced countries the participation of women in the labour market has increased significantly, Italy continues to lag behind most of them. In the lower classes it is especially the case that the birth of a child induces women to stay at home, because the cost of external child care is too high (see Chapter 5). It is also true that the low propensity of most Italian men to help with family duties is an additional factor discouraging women's employment. Column 3 of Table 3.2 shows that rates of unemployment in Italy have only been low during the economic miracle years, primarily a sign of the general difficulty of the Italian economy to generate enough jobs, but also indicative of a black economy that offers additional jobs not picked up by official statistics, although generally of poor quality. The employment situation worsened considerably after the 2008 crisis.

Some other features of the Italian labour market are reported in Table 3.3, where one can see the transformation of the Italian economy in the period covered in this book. In 1951 Italy still had 9 million people working in agriculture, while today there are less than 1 million. As we've already noted (Chapter 2), 5 million people left agriculture between 1951 and 1971 and a further 3 million later. Industrial employment did increase to a peak of 7.5 million workers in 1981 (although the peak was reached in the early 1970s), but then the sector has slowly lost jobs, most rapidly after 2008 (something that I will return to in Chapter 4). Employment in services instead has continued to grow, as in all other advanced economies. Italy occupies a middle-ranking position in terms of number of hours worked (column 4), contrary to popular assumptions (namely, that Italians don't work hard), while column 5 shows the high level of worker disputes between the 1960s and 1980s, followed by a major decline in strike activity. The peak in labour conflicts was reached in 1969–79, with an average of 49 million working hours lost per year (for post-1968 events, see Chapter 2).

Table 3.3 Employment: sectors and working hours, 1951–2011

	% Labour force			Yearly working hours per worker	Hours of work lost per year thousand
	Agriculture	Industry	Services		
	1	2	3	4	5
1951	44.3	31.0	24.8	na	8,668
1961	31.3	36.0	32.7	na	20,196
1971	19.8	37.0	43.2	na	35,844
1981	12.2	35.9	51.8	1,888	22,129
1991	6.9	30.1	63.1	1,856	2,546
2001	4.6	27.6	67.8	1,794	2,325
2011	3.8	25.4	70.8	1,778	1,038

Source: my elaborations from Giordano, Zollino, 2015 and Istat

INCOME, PRICES AND PRODUCTIVITY

As we have seen, the Italian economy grew at a fast rate during the economic miracle, and then growth rates slowed down, as can be seen in Table 3.4. In the years 1974–92 however, the average growth rate still remained slightly ahead of growth rates in the United States and the process of catching up continued, albeit at a slower pace. In the years 1993–2007, however, the Italian economy started to lag behind, albeit marginally, but then the world crisis hit Italy severely. Between 1951 and 1971 Italian per capita GDP had trebled, while between 1971 and 2007 it had doubled. In 2016, the per capita level of income is still only 91 per cent of what it had been in 2007.

This peculiar path of the Italian economy, which showed the capability to catch up with the leading world economies for many years, and which has now revealed great difficulties in keeping pace with globalization, can be appreciated in Figure 3.1, where it is possible to follow the yearly

Table 3.4   Per capita GDP growth rates, 1951–2016

1951–1973	5.0
1974–1992	2.1
1993–2007	1.5
2008–2016	-1.1

Source: my elaborations from A. Baffigi, 2015; data are updated to 2016 from official sources.
Note: computed from chained values

Figure 3.1   Per capita GDP at 2016 prices, 1951–2016

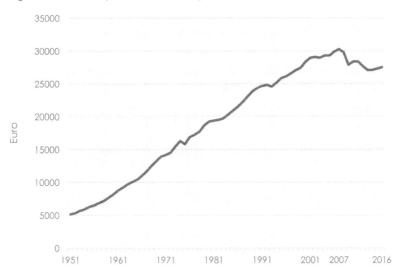

Source: Baffigi 2015

changes in per capita GDP at 2016 prices. I have offered a preliminary explanation for this in Chapter 2: a too high level of public debt, accumulated in the 1980s, prevented the massive use of fiscal measures to reflate the domestic economy after the crisis, and instead induced major cuts in public investments; and the lack of international competitiveness on the part of too many small businesses saw countless bankruptcies during the crisis. These negative economic factors were accompanied by political turmoil, which delayed the necessary reforms.

We can follow in Table 3.5 other details of the evolution of GDP. Column 4 shows the shrinking of the agricultural sector, while in column 5 we see that value added (VA) in industry, already quite important percentage-wise in 1951, marginally enlarged, but then started shrinking in relative terms from 1986. The great enlargement of VA in services followed the established pattern of advanced countries. A comparison between imports and exports of goods and services shows an approximate balance (we shall examine the foreign sector in more detail below). Finally, column 10 shows that investments, both private and public, were particularly high during the economic miracle and then decreased to reach an extremely low level. A glance at the rates of inflation in Table 3.6 reveals that Italy only had a burst of inflation in the 1970s–early 1980s, at the time of the two oil crises and at the height of the Red Brigades, events that challenged the stability of the country. Otherwise, rates remained quite low, although sometimes not as low as in other European countries (particularly Germany).

The slowdown of the rate of growth of Italian income before the crisis and then the decline after has had a devastating impact on the position of Italy *vis-à-vis* other advanced countries. We can see in Table 3.7 what happened. Italy had a per capita GDP in 1995 (the earliest year in the Eurostat data bank for this indicator) 21 per cent higher than the EU average, only 8 percentage points below Germany and above France and the UK, while Spain was 30 percentage points adrift. In 2007 Italy had already lost 14 percentage points, but it was still above the EU average. During the crisis, Italy lost another 11 points, falling below the EU average, while France,

Table 3.5 GDP composition, 1951–2015 (absolute values in billion euros)

	GDP at factor costs	GDP at market prices	Total resources	Agriculture	Industry	Services	Imports	Exports	Consumption	Investments
	1	2	3	4	5	6	7	8	9	10
1951	6	6	7	24.0	33.1	35.8	11.2	9.7	71.8	18.4
1961	12	14	16	15.6	37.4	47.0	11.8	11.9	64.3	23.8
1971	35	39	45	8.5	37.7	53.9	13.2	14.1	65.3	20.7
1981	232	244	304	5.8	36.5	57.7	19.5	18.1	62.1	19.8
1991	699	769	905	3.7	30.6	65.6	14.9	15.2	66.0	18.8
2001	1,093	1,256	1,576	2.9	27.3	69.7	20.3	21.4	62.1	16.5
2011	1,374	1,580	2,058	2.4	24.7	73.0	23.2	22.1	62.7	15.2
2015	1,402	1,645	2,091	2.1	19.2	74.6	21.3	23.6	63.2	13.2

Source: values in lire until 1998 have been transformed in euros at the exchange rate of December 1998 1936,27 lire per 1 euro.

GDP at market prices = GDP at factor costs + indirect taxes

Total resources = GDP at market prices + imports

% sectoral value added is computed on GDP at factor costs

% imports, exports, consumption and investments is computed on total resources

Source: see table 3.4

the UK and Spain had also fallen back, they did so less and only Germany remained more or less at the same comparative level. Whereas Austria, the Netherlands and Sweden showed themselves as the most stable European economies. These figures summarize vividly the drama of the Italian economy over the past 20 years: only Japan among the advanced countries has fared (a little) worse.

Table 3.6 Average annual rates of inflation, 1956–2015 (%)

1956–1960	2.4
1961–1965	5.0
1966–1970	3.2
1971–1975	13.7
1976–1980	17.2
1981–1985	11.3
1986–1990	5.7
1991–1995	4.6
1996–2000	2.1
2001–2005	2.4
2006–2010	1.9
2011–2015	1.3

Source: Istat

Productivity is best measured in terms of GDP per hour worked rather than GDP per worker, which can be skewed by differences across countries in yearly hours worked and in the employment rate. Italy's productivity benefited from the catching up process that continued until the early 1990s. As can be seen in Table 3.8, in 1995 Italy stood at a level of 123 per cent of the EU average, while Germany was at 131, France at 136 and the United States at 131;[3] the UK was far below Italy. Then things went wrong. Productivity dropped many percentage points before the crisis,

Table 3.7   Comparative per capita GDP, 1995–2015 (EU=100)

	1995	2003	2007	2011	2015
Italy	121	111	107	104	96
Germany	129	116	117	123	124
France	116	111	108	108	106
Spain	91	98	103	93	90
Netherlands	123	129	138	133	128
Austria	134	128	124	128	128
Sweden	125	124	128	126	124
UK	113	122	111	105	108
USA	159	156	152	144	145
Japan	129	112	106	99	99

Source: Eurostat

Table 3.8   Comparative productivity GDP per hour worked, 1995–2015 (EU=100)

	1995	2003	2007	2011	2015
Italy	123	107	105	104	101
Germany	131	126	127	126	126
France	136	136	131	129	128
Spain	111	101	99	97	97
Netherlands	132	133	138	130	127
Austria	122	114	114	113	118
Sweden	118	118	124	118	115
UK	105	113	107	102	99
USA	131	134	134	136	138
Japan	77	80	78	75	73

Source: Eurostat

while during the crisis productivity only stabilized (as a counterbalancing factor, unemployment increased). Table 3.9 shows the gaps in income per capita across the Italian areas and helps to explain how Italy could remain competitive in spite of what we have seen above.

Table 3.9 Regional differences in per capita GDP, 1951–2011

	Nominal				
	1951	1971	1991	2001	2011
	1	2	3	4	5
North-West	152	129	124	123	121
North-East	106	105	117	118	118
Centre	102	105	109	108	112
South	61	71	70	68	68
ITALY	100	100	100	100	100

Source: E. Felice, 2015

	Deflated for different areas purchasing power				
North-West	149	123	113	115	112
North-East	112	111	117	116	117
Centre	91	92	103	103	106
South	65	80	80	79	78
ITALY	100	100	100	100	100

Source: G. Vecchi, 2011

The key to understanding this is precisely Italy's regional gaps, not only in per capita income, but also in productivity and unemployment (not shown here). Regional gaps, an historical legacy, were extremely large in 1951. A sustained process of catching up on the part of the North-East and central regions had taken place, especially after the economic miracle, when SMEs started to become assertive in the wake of the third industrial revolution, while the North-West showed less than average performance. If we separate the North-East region from the centre, we can see that the North-East had caught up by 1991 if we use data deflated for differentials in cost of living; after 1991 the North-West and North-East remained aligned. The centre was much further behind in 1951 and produced a more spectacular improvement, remaining at some distance from the North, more pronounced if we use deflated data. The South, instead, shows an aborted process of convergence[4] stopping in the 1970s, with a slight worsening thereafter. However, what is worth underlining here is that the use of deflated data boosts the results for the South substantially (of around 10 percentage points), because the cost of living was substantially lower than in the rest of the country. If we consider that the South enjoys a substantial amount of social transfers from the North (something that will be analysed later), it becomes clear that the South has actually improved its standard of living substantially, while gaps remain high in the production of good jobs (employment and productivity).

In terms of Italian competitiveness, the conclusion that can be drawn from this regional data is that competitiveness in industry, mostly located in the North of the country, is higher than the Italian average. It should also be said that since the crisis much of the industry outside the strong areas of the North has disappeared. This brings us to the discussion of international trade.

FOREIGN TRADE

About one quarter of Italian GDP is exported and about the same is imported. Today, international trade, as a percentage of GDP is more than double that of 1951, showing the strategic role it has played in Italian economic growth. Table 3.10 shows that the balance of trade (in goods and services) has not always been positive. In particular, Italy is very sensitive to the price of raw materials, especially oil and gas, because it cannot count on its own reserves. The oil shocks of 1973–4 and 1981 both

Table 3.10 Balance of payments in Italy, 1971–2015

						(million euros at current prices)		
	1971	1981	1991	2001	2007	2011	2015
Exports	6,229	55,013	137,099	338,264	448,237	453,195	493,751
Imports	5,936	59,897	136,350	321,125	451,936	476,790	443,094
Balance of Trade	293	-4,884	749	17,139	-3,699	-23,595	50,657
Net income and transfers	207	-748	-16,362	-13,561	-24,420	-24,545	-24,008
Net capital account	-12	79	378	936	2,260	486	2,638
BOP current account	**488**	**-5,553**	**-15,235**	**4,514**	**-25,859**	**-47,654**	**29,287**
Net BOP Financial account	na	na	19,528	-2,889	26,131	72,845	25,605
Balance of Payments	na	na	4,293	1,625	272	25,191	54,892

Source: my elaborations from Istat and Bank of Italy sources

produced a short-term trade deficit, while the years 1985–92 showed a deficit produced by the excess of public spending, redressed later. The years, 2008 to 2012 saw a mismatch between exports (stable) and imports (slowly increasing), but since 2013, exports have picked up again, while imports have been restrained by the fall in domestic demand, restoring a comfortable balance of trade surplus.

Italy's balance of payments current account has been increasingly burdened by transfers made by immigrants to their home countries, while the capital account has generally remained positive. The financial account has also in the main remained positive. Although Italy does not have a problem of persisting deficits in its balance of payments, being still today a large producer and exporter of industrial products, and showing a large surplus in the tourism sector, it does not enjoy the huge balance of payments surpluses of Germany, the Netherlands, Denmark and Sweden, because of its large imports of energy. It is worth noting however that France, Spain and the UK all have much larger and more persistent balance of payments deficits than Italy, not to mention the United States, which has continued to run a deficit for the last three decades. We shall look more closely at the composition of Italian exports in Chapter 4.

THE PUBLIC SECTOR

During the economic miracle, Italy had low public expenditure and low public debt. A universal welfare system was not yet in place, as can be seen in Table 3.11 from the extremely low social expenditure for 1961. By 1981 social expenditure had substantially increased, but public debt was nevertheless still under control. It was in the 1980s and early 1990s that the public deficit exploded, as I have explained in Chapter 2, because revenues did not keep pace with expenditures in the presence of a concomitant cut in inflation due to Italian participation in the EMS. When Italy exited the EMS in 1992, Italian governments were finally persuaded by the financial attacks on the lira to control public finances, resulting in a shrinking of deficits and public debt until 2003, greatly helped by a series of privatizations. Public debt had reached a plateau by 2007, but then experienced a new rise with the ensuing financial crisis. This increase in public debt during the crisis was more contained than in most other European countries, but it started from an already very high level. The yearly changes of debt as a percentage of GDP can better be viewed in Figure 3.2, where the steep rise in the 1980s is clearly seen. In Table 3.11, the efforts to restrain public debt can be appreciated in column 4, which shows the so-called "primary balance", the state budget balance excluding interest payments on public debt. This primary balance was heavily negative in the 1970s and 1980s in conjunction with the lavish public spending of the time; thereafter it remained positive, more so in the years in which public debt shrunk before the crisis. Italy has, therefore, been maintaining a surplus in public finance for over two decades, including the crisis years, without putting public debt under control, which would have entailed an even higher primary balance.

Table 3.11 Public expenditure and debt, 1961–2015

	(% of GDP)				
	Total public expenditure	Social expenditure	Deficit	Primary balance	Public debt
	1	2	3	4	5
1961	25.7	7.8	0.2	1.3	31.0
1971	35.6	12.5	-2.5	-1.6	53.0
1981	45.3	20.1	-10.9	-5.8	61.5
1991	54.3	22.4	-11.4	0	98.0
2001	48.1	24.1	-3.1	3.2	108.8
2007	48.4	25.7	-3.7	3.5	103.5
2011	49.4	28.5	-3.5	1.2	116.5
2015	50.4	30.0	-2.6	1.6	132.0

Source: my elaborations from Istat and Francese & Pace 2008

Figure 3.2 Public debt as a percentage of GDP, 1951–2016

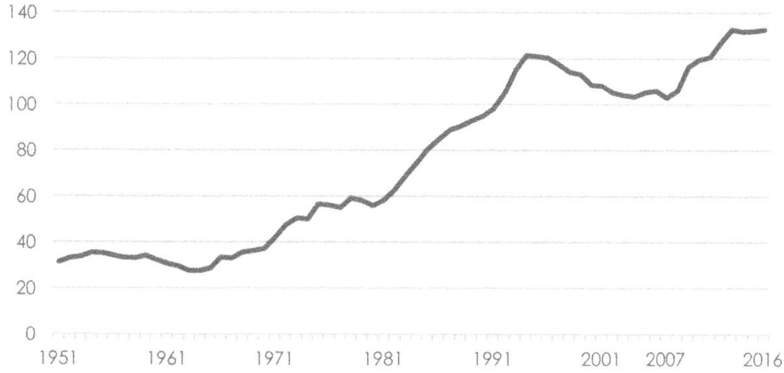

Source: Francese & Pace 2008

One cannot maintain that Italy has been unwilling to raise taxation. Since 1975, tax rates have increased by 18 percentage points of GDP, while the OECD average has only increased 4 percentage points (9 percentage points in France, 3 percentage points in Germany). Italian public finance faces three key challenges: 1) tax evasion: the "tax-gap", the gap between tax rates and tax revenues can be estimated today at around 15 per cent, with a predominance in retail trade and other services.[5] It is particularly difficult to evaluate tax evasion in Italy because of the highly fragmented character of Italian business, which makes controls exceedingly costly. Efforts at increasing controls have produced some results, but have not eradicated the problem. 2) the black economy: most of the tax evasion is concentrated in the black economy, which has been estimated at one quarter of Italian GDP (criminal economy included), higher than the OECD average.[6] 3) the slow administration of justice, which does not favour tax compliance.

We can say, therefore, that the country's fiscal capacity is low, but paradoxically those who do pay taxes pay very high taxes. In personal taxation, there is no specific provision to support families with children, for whom there are only limited deductions. Italy's very low fertility rate is

71

also blamed on this lack of fiscal support. This picture is further complicated by the unbalanced structure of taxation: Italy has an extremely high rate of personal taxation and of revenues coming from this single source, with dependent workers paying much more than independent ones. As social contributions have increased, which are deducted from wages by employers, this too has further contributed to the reduction in the size of the worker's pay packet. Taxes on property and wealth, however, are low, while indirect taxes (VA taxes) are subject to an extremely high rate of tax evasion (according to an IMF estimate, only 41% of what should be collected from this source actually enters the state coffers – 58% is the OECD average). A rebalancing of the tax structure is long overdue. Recent governments have tried to cut the rate of tax here and there, but such attempts run counter to the needs of rebalancing state budgets and public debt and so could not be substantial.

THE WELFARE STATE

The Italian welfare state was reorganized and made universal in the 1970s, as we have seen in Chapter 2, and as a percentage of GDP is above the EU average (see Figure 3.3). But it shows very distinctive features, being both heavily weighted in favour of the elderly and ineffective in lifting people out of poverty. Table 3.12 shows the composition of social benefits by function and shows how expenditure on pensions eclipses all other benefits (although showing a slight percentage reduction over recent years). The pensions burden on GDP has gone from 8.2 per cent in 1974 to 14.7 per cent in 1994, essentially as a result of the increase in life expectancy and the increase in the share of the population over 60. Legislation that made it easier to qualify for pensions also contributed to the pension burden until the beginning of the 1990s. Since then, numerous reforms of the pension system have been enacted, which have progressively succeeded in restraining pensions, so that 20 years later, in 2015, the impact of pensions expenditure on GDP had only increased 2.5 percentage points to 17.2 per cent, due primarily to a postponement of the retirement age and

Figure 3.3 Comparative total expenditure on social protection, 2013 (as a percentage of GDP and PPS per capita)

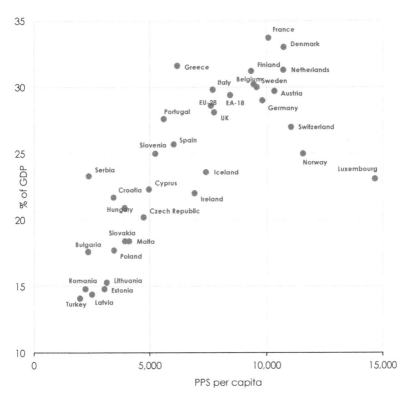

Source: Eurostat
Note: EU-28, EA-18, Greece, Poland: 2012 data; Denmark, Germany, Spain, France, Italy, Latvia, Lithuania, the Netherlands, Slovenia, Slovakia, Sweden, UK and Turkey: provisional data.

the move from a defined benefits to a defined contributions payment scheme.[7] This, however, has not prevented average pension income from growing substantially, because none of the reforms has introduced a cap to publicly-funded pensions. Between 2003 and 2014 new state pensions (2.5 million) rose on average from €14,000 to €23,000 per year. Although there is a backlog of low pensions, these are being substituted by higher ones. In 2015, the average pension was €17,323 per year for the 16 million retired people: however, this figure disguises the fact that 40 per cent got less than €1,000 per month and 39 per cent got less than €2,000. The 21 per cent of retired people getting more than €2,000 per month has absorbed 44.6 per cent of the total public expenditure for pensions (amounting to €280 billion).

Table 3.12 Composition of social benefits by function, 2003–2014 (%)

	2003	2007	2014
Health care	25.0	25.9	23.5
Disability	5.8	5.7	5.9
Elderly	62.6	59.0	58.6
Family and children	4.0	4.4	5.4
Unemployment	1.8	4.3	5.8
Other	0.8	0.7	0.8

Source: Eurostat

Italy's second largest item of social expenditure is its health service. As we can see from Table 3.13, per capita expenditure on health services is the lowest among those countries listed, while life expectancy is the second highest, just below Japan. Indeed, in 2017 the Bloomberg Global Health Index, comparing 163 countries, ranked Italy as the healthiest country on earth. Obviously, health has determinants that go well beyond health services. It is well known that 40–50 per cent of good health is due to socio-economic factors, chiefly a healthy diet, regular exercise, and a lack of vices known to jeopardize health (drugs, smoking, alcohol); another 20–30 per cent is due to the environment, a further 20–30 per cent is genetics, and only 10–15 per cent is down to health services in the narrow sense. Indeed, Figure 3.4 shows that there is an inverse relation between per capita expenditure on health services and life expectancy, showing quite clearly that other factors are more important in supporting health. The Italian "Mediterranean" diet is healthy – high in vegetables, fruit, whole grains, legumes and olive oil. Italy's smaller and older cities facilitate walking and cycling; and the landscape of hills, mountains and lakes provide ample opportunities for physical exercise and open air sports and recreation all year round, encouraged by Italy's mild climate. As for the influence of genetic legacies, Italy has notable areas (Sardinia and Calabria, mostly) with above average levels of centenarians, which has been the focus of international research. None of this is to minimize the contribution made by the Italian health service, which is well organized, technologically advanced and available to every citizen.[8]

Table 3.13 Comparative life expectancy and health expenditure, 2014

	Life expectancy years	Per capita expenditure on health ($)
Japan	84	3703
Italy	83	3258
France	82	4959
Germany	81	5411
UK	81	3935
Canada	82	5292
USA	79	9403

Source: World Bank, *World Development Indicators*

These two welfare expenditure items dwarf any other social expenditure. As unemployment increased over the crisis years, state benefits also increased, but mostly for those who lost a permanent job. Most other unemployed did not receive any relief. What is important to note is the very modest support offered to families by the Italian welfare state.

Traditionally, this has been due to the fact that Italian families provided the bulk of childcare, either because women withdrew from work after having children or because grandparents (mostly grandmothers) provided most childcare needs. But this pattern has become increasingly dysfunctional in a context in which mothers wish to continue working and where grandparents themselves are increasingly engaged in work. This has certainly contributed to the fall in birth rates.

Figure 3.4 Relation between per capita health expenditure and life expectancy, 2014

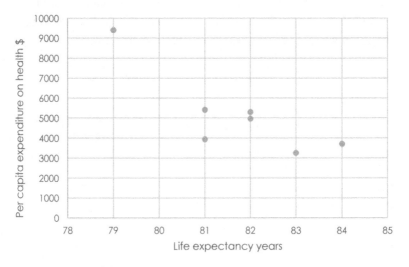

Source: World Bank, World Development Indicators.

Table 3.14 shows the level of poverty and severe deprivation, where poverty is defined as the percentage of people with a per capita income below 60 per cent of the median disposable income, and severe deprivation as not being able to meet even a basic standard of living. It can be seen that in Italy, and in Spain and Sweden, the situation, *before* social transfers, had worsened since the 2008 crisis. Interestingly, *after* social transfers had been made, with the exception of the UK, all countries had higher rates

Table 3.14 Comparative poverty rates, 2008 and 2015

	% of population				
	2008		2015		2015
	social transfers		social transfers		deprivation
	before	after	before	after	severe
France	18.5	12.5	17.7	13.6	4.5
Germany	20.1	15.2	20.0	16.7	4.4
UK	23.2	18.7	23.5	16.7	6.1
Sweden	14.9	12.2	16.0	14.5	0.7
Spain	23.8	19.8	28.6	22.1	6.4
Italy	25.5	18.9	28.7	19.9	11.5
North-West			18.5	11.8	7.0
North-East			15.9	9.9	4.8
Centre			24.0	16.1	8.4
South			44.3	32.0	18.6
Islands			50.8	38.2	24.2

Source: Eurostat

of poverty than in 2008, which seems to imply a difficulty on the part of social expenditures to cushion market difficulties. Only Spain performs less well than Italy as a whole, but it is interesting to compare the values for each of the Italian regions. The North of Italy has a lower percentage of poverty than Sweden, particularly the North-East (but not in the severe deprivation index) and the centre is comparable to Germany and the UK (but again not in the severe deprivation index). The real problem is clearly the South and islands, showing values comparable only to those of some of the Eastern European countries. This varied picture is confirmed also by the Gini coefficients reported in Table 3.15 and calculated on equivalized disposable income, income after taxes and transfers. Taken as a whole Italy ranks highly in terms of inequalities, but when the country is broken down by territory, one can see that the North and centre perform in line with France and Germany (Sweden has a distinctly lower level of inequality), while the South and islands have much higher values and share company with Spain.

Table 3.15 Comparative Gini coefficients of equivalized disposable income, 2007–15

	2007	2012	2015
France	26.6	30.5	29.2
Germany	30.4	28.3	30.1
UK	32.6	31.3	32.4
Sweden	23.4	24.8	25.2
Spain	31.9	34.2	34.6
Italy	32.0	32.4	32.4
North-West		30.1	
North-East		27.9	
Centre		30.5	
South		33.7	
Islands		34.2	

Source: Eurostat and Istat

The structure of the Italian welfare state favours the middle classes over those in real poverty and privileges old people over young, who are disadvantaged both by the modest benefits provided to families, and by the very high youth unemployment rate. If we add to this the precarious nature of many of the contracts young people receive for their first jobs and the low pay offered by many of the service jobs available, we can easily understand why the present conditions of young people in Italy are so unsatisfactory. Istat has in its 2016 annual report shown that relative poverty at the end of the 1990s was higher among people over 65 years of age than among people below 17 years (16% versus 12%), but that the relative poverty of the over 65s has declined to 10 per cent in 2014, while that of the under 17s has shot up to 19 per cent between 2011 and 2014. No surprise that young Italians are increasingly escaping abroad (see Chapter 5). Italian governments began in 2013 to introduce measures to soften these perverse implications of the welfare system, by introducing various benefits for low-income citizens, but the real counterbalancing force remains the Italian family, which has been ready to offer support to children and grandchildren.

THE LIRA, THE EUROPEAN MONETARY SYSTEM AND THE EURO

At the end of the Second World War, Italy had an extremely high rate of inflation, which the governments of the newly born republic sought to bring under control. In 1947, on the eve of Italy's participation in the Marshall Plan, steps were taken by Luigi Einaudi[9] to stabilize the lira – the "linea Einaudi" ("Einaudi approach") – public deficits were brought under control, interest rates and banks' reserve requirements were raised. Italy was then ready to enter the gold exchange standard, and after the general round of adjustments of exchange rates imposed by the IMF in 1949, the Italian lira became fixed at 625 lire per US dollar until the demise of the gold exchange standard in the early 1970s. Throughout the 1950s and 1960s monetary policies remained orthodox, public deficits minimal and public debt low. Indeed, historically, Italy had a record of monetary stability, having been able to stay within the classical gold standard between 1881 and 1914, notwithstanding some temporary difficulties, and was able to revert to the gold standard in 1926 with Mussolini. The troubles of the 1970s, however, caused by the international and domestic factors outlined in Chapter 2, pushed the government of the time to unleash inflation and let public budget deficits enlarge,[10] with an inevitable devaluation of the lira.

In the second half of the 1970s, the European Union reconstructed a system of fixed, but adjustable, exchange rates – the European Monetary System (EMS) – and Italy was faced with the choice of whether or not to adhere to this new step of European integration. Having been a founding member of the EU, it was considered impossible not to participate and in March 1979 Italy entered the EMS. At that point, inflation had to be brought under control, something that was achieved in 1981 through the "divorce" between the Bank of Italy and the Treasury, whose commitments could no longer be financed without limits by printing money, a decision already explained in Chapter 2. Unfortunately, as budget deficits were not brought under control, public debt exploded (see Table 3.11) and speculation forced Italy out of the EMS in September 1992. Meanwhile, in December 1991, at Maastricht the EU had agreed, with Italy's participation, to move from the EMS to Economic and Monetary Union (EMU) including a common currency. The Italian economy, however, did not measure up well against the indicators required by the Maastricht agreement and again the country was faced with a decision, whether or not to join the EMU. Once more, it was not politically acceptable for Italy to remain outside and the Prodi government, as we have seen, proceeded towards meeting the required indicators, with the exception of public debt, which remained far above the required 60 per cent. In consideration of the fact that Italy had been part of all the steps of European integration, the country was accepted into the EMU, under the promise that it would reduce its public debt through a process of privatization.

In December 1998, the Italian lira was fixed against the new common currency – the euro – at 1,936.27 lire per euro. No longer would the country be able to use devaluations to recover competitiveness, to let inflation go higher than in neighbouring countries, and to accumulate public deficits and public debt without limits. As I have made clear, Italy had not been prone to mismanagement of its public finances, or to high rates of inflation, in the years of the economic miracle in which it "played by the rules" of monetary and fiscal stability inside the gold exchange standard without any negative impact on growth. But the tendency to use easy monetary policies and deficit spending, as Italy had done since the middle of the difficult 1970s, conflicted with the binding constraints imposed as a result of choosing to remain inside the European framework (first by entering the EMS and then by joining the single currency) and Italy's governments have proved incapable of resolving this tension effectively.

What has happened to Italy inside the Eurozone can be explained in this context. Before 1996, when the lira could no longer be devalued to re-enter the EMS (which was one of the conditions for the participation in EMU), devaluations had helped many Italian small businesses to remain competitive, in spite of their technological and organizational inadequacy when faced with globalization. With EMU in place, many of these small businesses could no longer survive and the rate of growth of Italian GDP started to contract, while public debt showed some decrease as a result of privatizations. The adjustment of the Italian economy was able to continue without major disruption, but when the financial crisis arrived this accelerated enormously the bankruptcies of small businesses, without the Italian government being able to intervene with public spending to support investments and to redirect Italian industry towards consolidation and improved competitiveness, because the high level of public debt prevented any substantial expansionary measure.

At that point, EU austerity measures worked against Italy. Privatizations could no longer continue, public debt mounted again because budget deficits, although much smaller than in the past, were not counteracted either by extra revenues or by inflation, so investment plummeted, productivity stagnated, unemployment spread and domestic consumption contracted. Italy found itself in dire straits, although the wealth of its families remained high and exports remained above water. International investors and rating agencies began to deliver a negative verdict on the health of the Italian economy and started selling the Italian public bonds they had in their portfolio. This caused the rate of interest on the Italian public debt to rise to unbearable levels, so that at the end of 2011 the Berlusconi government – which seemed incapable of coping with the emergency – was substituted with a technocratic government led by Mario Monti, who introduced drastic measures to cut public spending still further in order to calm speculation against the Italian economy. Clearly, these measures were of no help in reviving domestic demand, and the growth rate of the Italian economy turned heavily negative.

At the EU level there were no initiatives to assist expanding the EU economy through investments, in spite of promises, and Italy had to get out of its troubles on its own. The only help came from the European Central Bank, headed by Mario Draghi, with its programme of quantitative easing. However, this was coupled with another measure – Banking Union (see Chapter 4) – which only led to further problems for Italy, because of the large amount of non-performing loans that its banks had accumulated over the crisis and which now had to be liquidated, and because of the introduction of the "bail in" mechanism, which forced the participation of shareholders and investors of banks in their losses. By 2017 the worst part of the adjustment of the Italian economy was over: Italian companies and banks had learned that it is imperative to grow larger (see Chapter 4); Italian governments had learned that they need to "play the rules of the game" and the European and world economies appear to be entering a phase of expansion. What has yet to be straightened out is Italy's public debt, but if the economy continues to improve, as it seems to be doing, then a rational plan to solve that problem too should be achievable. After all, Italy has, in the past, been able to reduce its public debt, its levels of private debt are not nearly as high as other European countries, and overall Italy is not one of the most indebted nations of the world, as can be seen in Table 3.16.

In 2000, Italy had the highest level of public debt as a percentage of GDP among the countries reported in Table 3.16, but the lowest private debt. In 2007, public debt had remained more or less at the same level and private debt had increased slightly, but the total remained on a level comparable to other countries, with the exception of Japan, where

Table 3.16 Comparative public and private debt as percentage of GDP, 2000–2016

	2000			2007			2016		
	Public	**Private**	**Total**	**Public**	**Private**	**Total**	**Public**	**Private**	**Total**
France	58	177	235	64	200	264	96	234	330
Germany	59	171	230	64	200	264	71	148	219
Spain	58	190	248	36	275	311	99	207	306
UK	40	189	229	42	232	274	88	219	307
Japan	100	268	368	160	232	392	199	231	430
USA	58	181	239	62	211	273	106	200	306
Italy	**105**	**131**	**236**	**100**	**169**	**269**	**132**	**173**	**305**

Source: Eurostat and OECD

both forms of debt had exploded. By 2016, the situation had worsened everywhere, with the exception of Germany where total debt resided at a historical low, an indication of its low level of investment. When both public and private debt levels are combined Italy's debt level is on a par with that of the United States and the UK and lower than that of France. This observation should confirm Italy as not the insolvent country often portrayed, although certainly excessive reliance on state spending remains something to be brought under control. A focus on public debt alone, has however, hidden this truth.

THE QUALITY OF INSTITUTIONS

The effort to measure qualities and not only quantities is a recent trend and stems from two basic concerns: the need to complement GDP data, which, if used alone, tend to distort our understanding of both society and economy, and the need to limit arbitrariness in the judgement of qualitative aspects, especially when they impact on public life. Institutions have long been considered extremely relevant to the social and economic performance of countries and therefore it is no surprise that a large amount of the qualitative indicators recently produced by various agencies aim at measuring the quality of institutions, to compare their evolution across countries and over time. These indicators are based on a multiplicity of surveys, which are then averaged out. They seldom include "objective" indicators, but there is an overwhelming component of "subjective" opinion from people interviewed, particularly sets of "experts". These observations are not aimed at reducing the validity of these indicators, but at pointing out their limitations, because they do not cover all possible relevant aspects of the reality under concern and because local populations often learn how to bypass or neutralize malfunctioning institutions. Moreover, for a country like Italy, where a complicated cultural context makes it particularly difficult to do business, even on the part of Italians themselves, one might expect a generalized impression of the institutional context to be unfriendly and unfair.

After having warned about the limitations of these qualitative indicators, learning that Italy comes out very badly in almost all of them should give us cause for reflection. The most established indicator used is the World Bank's composite Worldwide Governance Indicator (WGI).[11] This indicator is a synthesis of six indicators: voice and accountability (freedom of expression and of the media); political stability and absence of violence (violence, terrorism); government effectiveness (quality of public services, of civil service); regulatory quality (promotion of private sector development); rule of law (confidence regarding contract enforcement, the functioning of courts and the likelihood of crime); and control of corruption. The ECB has produced a summary of the results for the countries of the Eurozone, but here we have returned to the original data and produced a comparison of only the largest countries (Table 3.17).

As Table 3.17 shows, Italy ranks in each category almost always last, although under political stability, it could be argued, unfairly. Where all countries have lost ground between 1996 and 2015 as a result of global challenges, it is puzzling to find Italy below the United States and Germany, where terrorist attacks have been much more evident than in Italy. Italy appears to have a low ranking because its governments typically last shorter terms than in most other advanced countries. However, Italy's low position in each of the other five indicators is quite understandable, and particularly disturbing in connection with both the rule of law and corruption indicators, which were already at a very low level in 1996 and have only worsened, considerably. There is no doubt that the slowness of the Italian legal and judiciary processes creates a negative perception about the actual quality of legal enforcement. I have mentioned in Chapter 2 that a reform of the justice system has been before the Italian parliament for the past three years and at the time of writing has only just been approved.

Italy is well aware of the fact that corruption is endemic in the country and even mounting. Partly this has to do with the older culture of distributing public contracts to existing businesses regardless of merit and efficiency, and partly with the diffusion of organized crime in some

Table 3.17 Comparative governance indicators, 1996 and 2015 (from −2.5 to +2.5)

	Voice and accountability		Political stability		Government effectiveness		Regulatory quality		Rule of law		Control of corruption	
	1996	2015	1996	2015	1996	2015	1996	2015	1996	2015	1996	2015
France	1.14	1.18	0.81	0.27	1.42	1.44	0.93	1.15	1.45	1.41	1.26	1.28
Germany	1.29	1.43	1.21	0.72	1.84	1.74	1.38	1.67	1.57	1.78	1.99	1.82
Italy	1.04	1.01	1.03	0.34	0.82	0.45	0.83	0.73	0.98	0.25	0.36	−0.05
Japan	0.89	1.02	1.11	0.98	0.96	1.79	0.69	1.18	1.32	1.51	1.05	1.61
UK	1.20	1.27	0.91	0.56	1.88	1.74	2.02	1.86	1.59	1.81	2.12	1.87
USA	1.36	1.08	0.87	0.70	1.71	1.46	1.59	1.30	1.45	1.60	1.57	1.38

Source: World Bank, *Wgi Data Set*

areas of the country. Italians have acted against corruption – the time of "clean hands" in 1992, which changed the political class in power and put in place, in 1996, an agency devoted to the control of public contracts, Autorità di Vigilanza sui Contratti Pubblici (AVCP). But it has not worked. A recent step forward has been the reorganization in 2017 of the existing anti-corruption agency into a new one, Autorità Nazionale Anti-Corruzione (ANAC), chaired by the former anti-mafia judge Raffaele Cantone. It is too early to evaluate whether the leadership of Cantone will strengthen this agency enough to actually reduce corruption effectively. Currently Italian citizens have the perception that corruption is prosecuted more often than before, but without a shortening of court procedures substantial results are unlikely to be achieved.

A regional analysis might shed some light on this shameful performance of the country in the institutional sphere. Table 3.18 does this. By selecting four of the WGI indicators (i.e. excluding both regulatory quality and political stability, which do not vary across regions) to produce a synthetic average (simple average, WGI-4), researchers have carried out an ad hoc survey by region of over 16 items connected with the 4 WGI indicators, which themselves have been averaged out to produce a synthetic indicator, that is then rescaled with the national averages of the WGI-4, to produce a regional variation comparable to the WGI indicators, called EQI.[12] The results for 2013 are shown in Table 3.18, showing each of the Italian regions, and in Figure 3.5, taken directly from the work quoted, it shows a picture for all European countries plus Turkey.

Both from the table and from the graph it can be seen that the quality of institutions index has a spread in Italy unmatched in any other country of the EU.[13] If we removed Latium (the city of Rome is notoriously corrupt and resembles the South rather than the rest of the country) and the South, Italy would reduce its negative average EQI by at least half, albeit still remaining the only "advanced" EU country showing a negative overall indicator. The extremely low value for Campania, only paralleled by a few regions of Bulgaria and Romania, corresponds to the region's bad reputation, despite it hosting some industrial excellence.[14]

Table 3.18 Quality of institutions (EQI) by region, 2013

France	0.59	ITALY	-0.91
Germany	0.82	*North*	
Spain	0.12	Piemonte	-0.64
UK	0.77	Val d'Aosta	0.63
Poland	-0.45	Liguria	-0.82
		Lombardia	-0.54
		Trento	1.00
		Bolzano	1.04
		Veneto	-0.19
		Friuli	0.37
		Emilia-Romagna	-0.22
		Centre	
		Toscana	-0.53
		Umbria	-0.49
		Marche	-0.54
		Lazio	-1.51
		South	
		Abruzzi	-1.10
		Molise	-1.66
		Campania	-2.24
		Puglia	-1.60
		Basilicata	-1.42
		Calabria	-1.69
		Sicilia	-1.59
		Sardegna	-1.31

Source: Charron, Dijkstra & Lapuente, 2015

Figure 3.5 Relation between EQI and growth rates in Italian regions, 2013

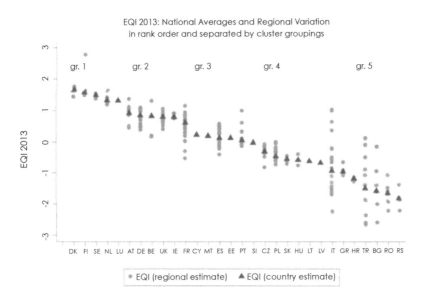

EQI 2013: National Averages and Regional Variation
in rank order and separated by cluster groupings

Source: see Table 3.18

What recent research has been trying to assess is whether low WGI (and EQI) indicators prevent economic growth, especially in a period of crisis, or prevent the consolidation of growth achieved before the crisis (both cases apply to Italy). ECB economists are convinced that this is the case on the basis of solid econometric evidence[15] and the pressing recommendation of the governor of the ECB Mario Draghi (and of the German authorities) to those Eurozone member countries that are not doing well in terms of growth rates to speed up their institutional reforms stems from this viewpoint. From a regional point of view, comparing the EQI indicators of Table 3.17 to the economic performance of the Italian regions in the last two decades, there is little doubt that both rankings (EQI and growth of income) see the North-East on top, followed by the North-West and the centre, while the South shows a distinctly poorer

Figure 3.6 Relation between EQI and cumulated growth rates for Italian regions, 2001–14

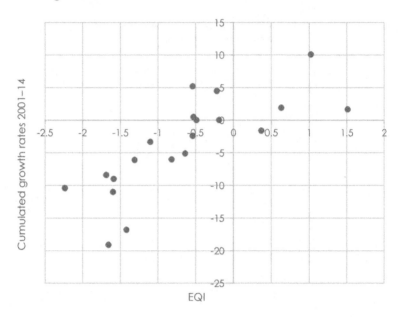

Source: Istat (and Table 3.17)

performance (see Figure 3.6). The correlation is obviously imperfect, because other variables are at work, but it lends further support to the need to improve institutions from the point of view of regional performance.

4

The form of the Italian economy

This chapter examines in more detail the nature of capitalism in Italy and its distinctive features, in particular its strong manufacturing specialization in hundreds of niche areas in which many Italian SMEs are world leaders. The "made in Italy" brand, a synonym for high quality and advanced design, does not comprise only of fashion, but also of other sectors of industry, mostly metal-engineering (see Table 4.1). Traditional industry (textiles, clothing and leather) declined from 31.4 per cent of the labour force in 1951 to 13 per cent in 2011, while over the same period metal and engineering products have risen from 30.1 per cent to 42.8 per cent. The impact of this shift on value added (VA) is even greater and, as we shall see, the impact on exports is overwhelming.

Big business in Italy is not widespread, and today is largely made up of the legacy of state-owned enterprises (SOEs), partly privatized. Table 4.2 shows the great "de-concentration" of Italian industry after 1971. In the years of the economic miracle, one quarter of the labour force worked in companies with more than 500 employees, while today it is only 10 per cent. There were 241 firms with more than 1,000 employees in 1991, with an average number of workers equivalent to 3,228; in 2011 that figure had reduced to 176 with an average of 2,438 workers, totalling only a little over 400,000 workers. The only two sizes of firm to have substantially enlarged over time are the 10–19 employees and 20–49 employees, while

Table 4.1   Manufacturing employment: composition by sector, 1951–2011

	1951	1971	1991	2001	2011
Food, beverages and tobacco	11.8	7.5	9.1	9.3	10.8
Textiles	18.8	10.1	7.7	7.6	3.6
Clothing	6.4	7.4	8.0	6.4	5.8
Leather	6.2	4.5	4.7	4.0	3.6
Wood and furniture	4.9	3.7	3.6	4.2	7.3
Paper and printing	3.6	4.1	5.4	5.3	4.3
Chemicals and pharmaceuticals	5.6	5.9	5.2	4.2	4.9
Rubber and plastics	1.0	2.4	3.4	4.5	4.6
Glass, cement, ceramics	5.6	6.3	5.3	5.2	5.1
Metals	4.8	5.0	3.3	3.0	3.2
Metal products	6.3	7.1	11.8	14.3	14.0
Machinery	8.6	13.8	10.3	12.3	11.9
Electrical machinery, electronics	4.3	7.4	9.1	9.5	7.1
Means of transport	6.1	6.6	6.7	5.5	6.6
Other	5.9	7.4	6.0	6.4	7.2
ALL	100.0	100.0	100.0	100.0	100.0

Source: Istat, Industrial censuses

those between 50 and 499 have fluctuated at around 30 per cent of the total. Today, the average size of a manufacturing firm in Italy is around 10 workers.[1] We should qualify this statement by recognizing that Italian entrepreneurs often prefer to build *groups* of smallish enterprises that are formally autonomous, rather than seek to merge their labour force into one single unit. This has only become apparent after the approval of legislation in 1991 that obliges companies to have a consolidated budget, but even after 1991, there are plenty of groups inside which there are companies that remain unconsolidated,[2] making it difficult to produce a precise quantitative analysis. By what means Italian SMEs have been able to remain competitive will be one of the subjects of this chapter.

Table 4.2 Manufacturing: size of firms, 1951–2011 (% of labour force)

	1951	1971	1991	2001	2011
1–9	32.3	20.2	26.2	25.8	26.4
10–19	5.4	8.7	15.3	15.9	15.3
20–49	8.7	13.1	16.3	17.4	17.4
50–99	8.1	10.8	10.0	11.3	11.4
100–199	11.8	10.4	9.1	9.9	10.6
200–499	8.6	12.8	10.1	10.0	9.4
>500	25.1	24.0	13.0	9.6	9.6
average size of firms	5.6	8.7	8.8	8.3	9.2

Source: Istat, Industrial Censuses

We shall give special consideration to the impact of both the 2008 financial crisis and the austerity policies that followed. In manufacturing particularly, the loss of employment was initially due to the international crisis, and the situation began to improve after 2009, but when the rest of the world continued to recover, Italy was faced with another crisis due to the fiscal stringency imposed by international speculation against Italian public debt (as we saw in the previous chapter), which caused a plummeting of domestic demand. Italian manufacturing was 14 per cent of the total manufacturing VA of the EU28 until 2009; in 2016 it was down to 11 per cent, and the loss was mostly due to the collapse in domestic demand. Companies which had opened up to international markets faced this second crisis much better than those that still catered solely for the home market.

NICHE CAPITALISM: INDUSTRIAL DISTRICTS
AND MEDIUM-SIZED ENTERPRISES

Since the 1960s it became apparent that SMEs in Italy were not disappearing because of the challenge of the American corporate model, but on the contrary they were reinventing themselves, especially in the North-East and centre. This phenomenon of "industrial districts" caught the attention of a number of economists in the 1970s and 1980s, including Giorgio Fuà,[3] a professor at the University of Ancona (Marche), but also active as a consultant for several companies; Giacomo Becattini,[4] a professor at the University of Florence, who elaborated a theory of "Marshallian districts" and Sebastiano Brusco,[5] a professor at the University of Modena (Emilia-Romagna), whose work was concerned with the measurement of the districts.[6]

The "industrial districts" have changed definition over time as their performance has, but they characteristically consist of local clusters of SMEs highly specialized in one basic product, manufactured in all possible versions and reliant on allied industries producing intermediate products and dedicated machinery. The proximity of firms allows the development of effective apprenticeships, often with the involvement of local universities, the establishment of multiple relations among firms, the organization of common services (including marketing), especially at the institutional level (research centres, show rooms, logistics), the creation of trust among businesses and a cultural predisposition to cooperation. As a result, these districts have built a sort of "social market" capable of diminishing transaction costs and of putting in place an effective division of labour inside the district rather than inside the single firm. Researchers have referred to a special "industrial atmosphere" developed in such places and to "positive external economies", that give rise to a specific pattern of growth: when a new phase of production is needed, it is done, not within already existing firms, but outsourced to somebody ready to set up a new firm, which remains in a tight relationship with the originator firm, but is formally autonomous.

Industrial districts started to be statistically analysed by Istat in the 1990s. In the 1991 census their number was fixed at 199, with 2.2 million workers and 42 per cent of total manufacturing employment. I have reported in Table 4.3 data from the 2001 and 2011 censuses, where the methodology was improved. In both years the districts accounted for 39 per cent of total manufacturing employment and 30 per cent of total turnover. However, it should be noted that Istat's definition does not include those concentrations of manufacturing specialism that are localized within cities where there is other manufacturing industries, for example, the "packaging valley" of Bologna, which specialized in packaging machinery, the historical leather district of Florence, and the "food valley" of Parma. Also "industrial districts" exist outside the manufacturing sector; for example, the "industrial" district of seaside tourism of Rimini and the mountain tourism specialism of Trento, Bolzano and Aosta. So, one can say that Istat's numbers under-report the importance of the cluster organization of business in Italy.

In any case, there are several things that can be learned from Table 4.3. Firstly, that the industrial districts could not escape the financial crisis, showing a fall in manufacturing employment in line with the entire manufacturing sector. However, if we look at the areas of specialization we can see that not all have followed the same trend: the districts of metal-engineering have increased their number and kept their employment constant overall;[7] those districts specializing in food and drink have doubled both in number and in employment; the chemical districts have remained unchanged, while all other sectors have seen contraction, with a lower level of impact only on the leather and shoes districts. It confirms what can be seen in Table 4.1, namely that over time, and especially across the crisis years, the heavy industry part of Italian manufacturing has resisted decline much better than light industry.[8] In particular, the fashion industry has shown an enormous decrease in levels of employment, chiefly as a consequence of the extensive offshoring of the most labour-intensive steps of production outside Italy, mostly in the Balkan countries and in Asia. Similarly, offshoring has been at the heart of the difficulties facing the

Table 4.3 Sectoral and regional distribution of industrial districts, 2001–11

	2001		2011		% change in workers
	No.	manufacturing workers	No.	manufacturing workers	
Textiles/clothing	45	537,435	32	386,335	-28.1
Leather, shoes	20	186,680	17	150,866	-19.2
Household appliances	32	382,332	24	179,656	-53.0
Jewellery, musical instruments	6	116,950	4	63,217	-45.9
Food	7	33,304	15	62,810	+88.6
Engineering, metal products	38	587,320	42	595,189	+1.3
Chemicals, rubber, plastics	4	48,585	5	45,350	-6.7
Paper and printing	4	35,996	2	21,067	-41.5
TOTAL	156	1,928,602	141	1,504,490	-22.0
North-West	39	799,420	37	570,552	-28.6
North-East	42	654,846	45	560,300	-14.4
Centre	49	383,857	38	295,644	-23.0
South	26	90,479	17	77,994	-13.8

Source: Istat

light industry industrial districts. Today, however, automation and robotics, coupled with an increase in the wages of Asian and East European workers, is giving rise to a "re-shoring" of many companies, particularly those producing high quality, high-tech products, reinvigorating many industrial districts. An informative and detailed comparison of the performance of firms over the duration of the crisis both inside and outside the industrial districts is provided by a survey of 149 industrial districts[9] by the research centre of Intesa-San Paolo. Turnover, profitability, productivity, exports, new patents were, for all size of firms, consistently better for those firms inside districts, with particularly good results for medium-sized firms, as we shall discuss below.[10]

The final piece of information offered by Table 4.3 is that the phenomenon of industrial districts is an overwhelmingly northern one, with a similar diffusion in both the North-West (mostly Lombardy) and the North-East (Veneto and Emilia-Romagna); the centre is also represented (Toscana and Marche), but there are only a few cases in the South.

Since 2009 an observatory of Italian industrial districts has been established and several legislative efforts at the local and central level have tried to "institutionalize" industrial districts in the areas of taxation and finance, but much more could be done. Before examining some qualitative aspects of these districts, there is one other important development that should be highlighted. The original and spontaneous growth of these clusters was ignited by firms that had grown out of the centuries old Italian crafts tradition catering for local demand, that become mechanized and thus capable of exporting to foreign markets. Since the 1990s, some of these firms became more substantial and more innovative than others giving rise to stratified clusters that hosted one or more leading firms, increasingly international, alongside the remaining smaller firms, which facilitated the flexibility of the system as well as guaranteeing most of the outsourcing needs. A value chain could be built that remained largely local but one that could be connected with international value chains. This change in the industrial districts was brought about by the internationalization required by globalization.

Although traditional industrial districts did not have difficulties in selling their products in international markets, none of the individual firms belonging to them was in a position to set up subsidiaries (commercial or productive) abroad and much less to buy foreign firms and become "multinational". Instead, these stratified industrial districts exhibited some medium-sized firms capable of internationalizing. As we saw in Chapter 2, these internationalized companies have been defined as "pocket multinationals". The strictly local networks of these firms have opened up to include other firms, thus losing part of their local dimension, while acquiring a worldwide presence and strategy. Italian clusters connect medium-sized and small-sized businesses, they rarely form part of Italian big business networks, due to, as we shall see, the limited confines of big business in Italy. Where a district is producing intermediate goods to be assembled by big business, rather than directly for consumers (like in the "fashion" districts), the importance of international value chains, typically dominated by foreign big business, becomes acute.

The definition of medium-sized firms is not precise and differs according to different sources. We will here adopt the definition used by the Mediobanca Research Centre,[11] which began in the 1990s the collection of data to monitor this new phenomenon. Medium-sized companies included in Mediobanca's data bank are those with between 50 and 499 workers and with a turnover between €16 million and €355 million. (There is also a second cluster surveyed of large-medium sized companies with a turnover below €3 billion and a work force of more than 500 employees.) Another requirement is that they must have Italian ownership. The number of enterprises in Mediobanca's dataset has changed over time: in 1996 it listed 3,383 enterprises, peaking just before the crisis at around 4,000, and by 2013 it was down to 3,212.[12] Their locality largely parallels that of the industrial districts, from which the medium-sized companies normally emerge, although there are some successful medium-sized companies that do not belong to the industrial districts, but are active in the same areas.

The reason why these firms have become the focus of study and are monitored is that over the twenty years between 1996 and 2016 they have performed better than the average, particularly during the crisis, and have become the most dynamic part of the industrial districts and of Italian industry at large. In the Unioncamere 2016 Report on medium-sized firms, it was revealed that between 2007 and 2014, all the indicators for the Mediobanca set of medium-sized firms were positive: +9.5 per cent in turnover and +13.4 per cent in value added; +25 per cent in exports (value); +8.7 per cent in productivity (while productivity in the Italian economy had overall declined) and +4.3 per cent in employment. Their sectorial distribution is shown in Table 4.4, where one can see that the sectors mirror those of the industrial districts. Two other observations worth highlighting: firstly, over the period of the crisis the importance of exports greatly increased as a result of shrinking domestic demand, and secondly, engineering, food and chemicals increased, while other sectors stagnated, engineering showing an extremely high propensity to export.

Indeed, it is in exports that Italian SMEs particularly performed: in 2015 the net balance of exports[13] by Italian manufacturing medium-sized companies was €98 billion (the German net balance of comparable companies was €100 billion). The enormous difference between the total net balance of €94 billion for Italy and that of €329 billion for Germany[14] was down to the impact of big business, which in Germany created a surplus of €229 billion and in Italy a €4 billion loss. While a discussion of the debacle of Italian big business is deferred to the next section, it is worth making some additional comments on the performance of exports. The recovery of Italian exports since the crisis has been substantial; the surplus of the balance of trade having reached €42 billion in 2014, €45 billion in 2015 and €52 billion in 2016, second only to Germany.[15] The work of economist Marco Fortis has deepened our understanding of where exactly Italy is more competitive in exports.[16] Working on UNCTAD/WTO data, which breaks down exports into 5,117 products, he has built several indicators for 2012 and 2014, which underline the "niche" nature of Italian capitalism. For example, if we take the absolute trade balance value for each product (raw materials from the energy sector excluded), Italy is first in

Table 4.4 Sectoral distribution of medium-sized enterprises, 1996–2013

	1996			2004			2013		
	No.	VA Billion euros	% exp	No.	VA Billion euros	% exp	No.	VA Billion euros	% exp
Engineering	1185	8.2	43.0	1506	13.1	44.1	1198	13.6	57.3
Metals	175	1.4	26.4	198	1.9	29.0	155	1.8	37.8
Fashion and household appliances	1045	6.6	38.9	1154	8.6	38.0	710	6.6	48.0
Food and beverages	413	2.9	14.3	476	4.0	17.2	467	5.0	23.8
Chemicals	335	2.5	29.3	431	4.0	33.0	433	5.0	39.0
Paper and printing	160	1.4	16.2	223	2.1	19.8	167	1.7	24.0
Other	70	1.3	33.0	94	0.7	30.0	82	0.8	39.0
TOTAL	3383	23.5	32.7	4082	34.4	34.2	3212	34.7	42.3

Source: F. Coltorti, *Medie imprese del settore meccanico elettronico*, 2014, www.mbres.it

235 products, second in 376 and third in 351, for a total of 932 products. In total these products produce a trade surplus of $177 billion. Normalizing this result per 100,000 inhabitants, Italy is second only to Germany, and ahead of all other countries. The distribution by sectors of the 235 products in which Italy is top (a total of $55.7 billion of net trade balance) sees engineering with 46 per cent of the total trade surplus, followed by fashion (33%), and food and drink (13%). Fortis has also constructed a more complex trade performance index, which also confirms for 2014 the same positioning of Italy (see Table 4.5). This analysis shows that Italy remains a competitive country with good chances for recovery if domestic demand can be reawakened.

Let us examine some of the better known niches of Italian manufacturing. The textile-clothing-leather industries have contracted over the last two decades, as we have seen in all tables, as a consequence of competition from China and other low-wage countries, but nevertheless still account for important clusters of high-level producers. The most famous Italian fashion brands[17] are many – Missoni, Valentino, Versace, Armani, Benetton,[18] Dolce e Gabbana, Roberto Cavalli, Prada, Gucci, Pucci, Max Mara, Marzotto, Ferragamo, Tod's, Geox, Fendi, Bulgari, Calzedonia, Piquadro – and there are many more flourishing in their niches. Their lasting success is connected with great creativity in the materials used, exclusive design and finishing quality.[19] They all benefit from a network of small businesses producing first-rate raw materials, like the tanned skin districts of S. Croce sull'Arno, Solofra, Vicenza or the silk district of Como. Connected to this kind of products, there is the district of Montebelluna producing ski-boots, skies and similar products, the spectacles district of Belluno, in which the most well-known company (today a very large one) was created by Leonardo del Vecchio. We can also mention the jewellery districts in the province of Vicenza, Arezzo and Valenza (Alessandria), and Marcianise (Caserta).

The household appliances and furniture sector depends on many districts in Marche, Veneto and Lombardia. One of the most curious specializations is the chairs district in Friuli, comprising some thousand small

Table 4.5 Country rankings, trade performance index (TPI), 2014

Sector	Germany	Italy	China	South Korea	Japan	France	USA	UK
Fresh food	25	33	49	82	97	25	5	42
Processed food	1	6	20	70	86	3	39	42
Wood products	1	25	36	44	54	30	33	36
Textiles	2	1	2	9	38	20	36	23
Leather, shoes	15	1	3	41	68	18	39	21
Clothing	18	1	2	50	87	14	47	20
Chemicals	1	28	25	7	8	2	20	34
Basic manufactures*	1	2	4	6	8	27	48	29
Non electronic machinery	1	2	5	10	12	11	25	14
Electronic components†	1	2	34	17	5	21	30	23
IT and consumer electronics	11	24	6	7	41	21	25	18
Transport equipment	1	2	27	3	13	16	33	31
Miscellaneous products‡	1	2	9	42	10	25	27	28
Minerals	30	46	76	62	84	25	18	32

* in metals, marble, ceramics

† home appliances included

‡ including jewellery, spectacles and plastic products

Source: Marco Fortis elaborations from UNCTAD-WTO data, in M. Fortis, 2016

Note: The TPI is calculated as a simple average of 5 indicators: 1. net exports; 2. per capita exports; 3. share of the world market; 4. product diversification; 5. market diversification

businesses, which together account for 20 per cent of global production. The sector is served by a meta-district of design employing some 50,000 people in six provinces of Lombardia. The "triangle of sofas" promoted by Pasquale Natuzzi between Basilicata and Puglia is another example of a successful niche district, this time outside of the usual location in the North-centre. In addition, there is the district of hotel equipment in Veneto, and ceramics, as well as marble, are generally processed in districts mostly in Veneto (Colli Euganei), Emilia-Romagna (Sassuolo, Faenza) and Toscana (Versilia, Massa e Carrara).

Food and wine is important throughout the country, but there are some significant districts: wine in Veneto in the provinces of Verona, Padova, Treviso and Vicenza (Soave, Bardolino, Prosecco), in Toscana and Piemonte (Canelli, Santo Stefano Belbo); cheese and ham in Parma and Reggio Emilia; fruit and vegetable production in Emilia-Romagna, Puglia, Campania and Sicilia; flowers in Liguria; the fishing districts of Mazara del Vallo (Sicilia) and Rovigo (Veneto).[20] Italy also has very old companies in the confectionary sector like the Pelino company (1783, Sulmona, Abruzzi) specializing in "confetti" (sugar almonds) or the Amarelli company (1731, Rossano, Calabria) making liquorice sweets. Panettoni (Christmas cakes), colombe (Easter cakes), chocolates, espresso coffee, traditional local sweets and cakes are all SME businesses throughout Italy.[21] One can also mention some important medium-large companies: Ferrero ("Nutella"), Barilla (pasta), Amadori (prepared meats), Conserve Italia (processed fruits and vegetables), Granarolo (dairy), Colussi (biscuits) and Lavazza (coffee).

The metal-engineering districts and its related mid-size firms are concentrated in Lombardia, Emilia Romagna and Veneto. Among its many districts are the packaging valley of Bologna; the motor valley of Bologna-Modena, where Ferrari, Lamborghini, Ducati and other luxury brands are located, as well as the production of farm machinery (Cento); the water fittings of Piedmont; the spare parts districts in Friuli, Piedmont, Lombardia and Emilia-Romagna; and various mechatronics districts in Lombardia, Veneto, Piemonte and Emilia Romagna. At the level of individual SME, firms range from Brembo, a large-medium sized company located in the province of Bergamo (Lombardia), that specializes in the production of brakes for the world's automotive industry, to Carpigiani in Bologna that has 50 per cent of the world market in machines producing ice-cream (*gelato*). Shipbuilding is located in Friuli and Liguria, where many of the best cruise liners are built. The aerospace district, producing spare parts, helicopters, satellites, space instruments, is in Lombardia, Piemonte, Lazio and Puglia.

A number of small chemical companies had grown up after the failure of Montedison in the 1990s (which we will discuss later), occupying interesting niches in the production of plastic commodities, focused particularly on trying to substitute oil as a raw material with raw materials of a vegetable nature. In pharmaceuticals, along with national niche producers many multinationals of Big Pharma have placed their productive plants for the European market in Italy, so that employment and production in the sector have not experienced much decline. Although, today Italy has a negative net balance in chemicals, because mid-size enterprises together cannot reach a high VA[22], the trade balance for pharmaceuticals is almost on a par.

The final point to be mentioned is the role of the family in running these medium-sized enterprises. This is a topic that commands a vast literature in Italy,[23] mostly for two reasons. Although family-run Italian SMEs have been highly successful in terms of quality and design, they have exhibited two problematic traits: the uneasy transition of management from one generation to the next, and the unwillingness to grow larger. Second and third generations have not always shown the same capabilities as the founder in the promotion of innovation and in the strategic decisions of a family company. Some of them have successfully brought in managers from outside, but often this has brought its own problems. One of the chief reasons family firms have shown a very low propensity to enlarge, is because families fear losing control of their company. Often when the inadequacy of the family management becomes apparent, these firms are sold, often to foreign businesses, and a very small part of them have become public. Another consequence of family ownership is that bank loans make up a disproportionate part of the capital of these companies, with a negative impact on banks' budgets when a crisis sets in (see below).[24]

BIG BUSINESS, SOES AND PRIVATIZATIONS

In 2011 the Italian economy had only 1,465 companies (0.03% of all enterprises) employing more than 500 workers, a total employment of 2.8 million (17% of total employment). In the same census, Istat also surveyed *groups* of enterprises, more than 90,000 in total, but only 1.5 per cent (1,350) of them reached more than 500 employees per group (with an average per group of 4,300 workers). Employment across these 1,350 groups totalled 3.2 million workers, or 20 per cent of total employment, only slightly more than the figure for single firms reported above. A thinner analysis would probably spot a strengthening of the medium-sized firms, often organized in groups.

In terms of turnover, if we use the Global 500 *Fortune* ranking, in 2015, it included only nine Italian companies (see Table 4.6). An analysis of these companies shows that six out of the nine were partially privatized SOEs. Two of the other three were insurance companies: Assicurazioni Generali, the largest of the Italian insurance companies, created in Trieste at the time of the Hapsburg Empire in 1831, and Unipol, which was founded by Italian cooperatives in 1963 to become the second largest insurance company in Italy.[25] The third is the Exor Group, controlled by the Agnelli family, heirs of Giovanni Agnelli, who in 1899 founded Fiat in Turin. It comprises Fiat Chrysler Automobiles (FCA),[26] (the world's eighth largest car manufacturer), Ferrari, CNH (a company producing agricultural, construction and industrial machinery), a real estate enterprise (Partner Re), the football team Juventus, as well as a 43 per cent stake in *The Economist*. Fiat, now part of Exor, with all its many supply chains outside the automobile industry, is a true anomaly in Italian economic history: it has always been a very large, privately owned, family controlled company (although with recent CEOs appointed from outside the family).[27] Precisely because it is an exception, Fiat commands a huge literature,[28] which illustrates also the role played by Fiat in Turin, in Piemonte and in Italy as a whole. With the "globalization" of Fiat in recent years, this local role has widely diminished and Turin is no longer the "company town" it once was, having succeeded in reinventing itself.

Table 4.6   Italian big business in *Fortune* Global 500, 2015

Ranking	Group	Revenues (billion $)
19	EXOR	153
49	Assicurazioni Generali	103
65	ENI	93
78	ENEL	84
224	Intesa-Sanpaolo	42
300	Unicredit	35
305	Poste italiane	34
404	Telecom Italia	27
491	Unipol	21

Source: Fortune Global 500, 2016

The disproportionate presence of former SOEs in the *Fortune* ranking is a good starting point to further discuss the issue of big business in Italy, because it opens up its most important chapter. We have already seen in Chapters 1 and 2 that the original bail-out operation by Beneduce of companies and banks after the 1929 crisis gave birth in 1933 to IRI, which remained in place until its liquidation in 2000. Telecom, Intesa San Paolo and Unicredit emerged from IRI, which included many more companies, none of which became so large as to be listed in Global 500 rankings, but nevertheless played an important role in Italian postwar economic growth.

We have also seen that the immediate postwar period saw the creation of ENI (in 1953) and that the centre-left governments in 1963 nationalized the electricity industry to create ENEL. All of these companies, therefore, belonged at one time to SOEs and have been partly or wholly privatized after 1992. As for Poste Italiane, this is a company still under state control today,[29] which has now greatly enlarged its financial side and competes directly with banks. To understand how these SOEs contributed to Italian economic growth is an important part of the story of the Italian economy in the postwar period.

IRI became a huge holding corporation for many companies organized into subholdings: Finsider (steel), Finmeccanica (engineering), Fincantieri (shipbuilding), Sme (food industries), Finmare (shipping), Autostrade (highways), Alitalia (air transport), Stet (telecommunications) and Finsiel (information technology).[30] Banks belonging to IRI, including Credito Italiano and Banca Commerciale Italiana, which formed the basis of Unicredit and Intesa San Paolo, were not placed in a subholding. Radio and later television broadcasting was also an IRI company. At the peak of its activity in 1980 IRI counted 570,000 employees and it had a share of total Italian GDP equal to 3.6 per cent. If we take into account only those sectors in which IRI was active, the share was equal to 6 per cent. IRI was also highly active in export markets as well as playing a significant role in investment in Italian infrastructure and transportation and Italy's advanced industries. It was widely used as the vehicle for the Italian government's developmental policies and investment in the South. During the years of the economic miracle, the consolidated budget of IRI was positive, turning profoundly negative in the years 1975–85, partly because of an insistence in enlarging capacity in a period of underutilization and partly because of inappropriate requests by the governments of the day (to maintain a higher than necessary labour force, to restrain price increases in periods of high inflation, and to absorb other failing enterprises).

With Finsider, Italy became the second biggest steel producer in Europe and built Europe's largest steel mill in Taranto. A high-level capacity in shipbuilding was provided by Fincantieri,[31] which remains in business, having merged with the French shipbuilding company Stx France in 2017. Finmeccanica (renamed Leonardo in 2016) presided over advanced engineering sectors, including helicopters, satellites, space instruments, defence electronics and armaments, and remains one of Italy's largest and most advanced industrial corporations.[32] STMicroelectronics, one of the world's largest producers of semiconductors and electronics components, was originally a company within Stet, then Finmeccanica, before becoming today an Italian-French company, jointly controlled, with a turnover of about €10 billion.

Two other groups from IRI are still in existence, but both are examples of unsuccessful privatization. One is Alitalia, which several governments have tried to privatize, with very poor results. The 2015 joint venture with Etihad looked like it had solved the company's problems, but that too ended in failure in 2017. Stet, in turn, relabelled Telecom in 1994, was privatized in 1997, with no effort by the state to find a suitable buyer. The company has continuously changed hands ever since, first held by Italian entrepreneurs, more recently by the Spanish company Telefonica and later by the French Vivendi, but at the time of writing its future remains unclear. The case of Telecom is widely considered the worst example of privatization in Italy's history.[33] It has prevented the company from growing and establishing itself internationally. Alongside Telecom we should also mention the steel plants of Finsider, which, when privatized, went to medium-sized Italian steel producers incapable of making the leap forward into big business and who, instead, led the plants to bankruptcy.[34] All the other pieces of the large IRI jigsaw have gradually been privatized, company after company, and no longer exist as groups, but before giving an overall assessment of the results of privatization, we should consider Eni, ENEL and Ferrovie dello Stato (FS), the Italian railways.

As shown in Table 4.6, Eni (Ente Nazionale Idrocarburi) is today a substantial oil company comparable in size to the Russian-owned Gazprom. At the beginning of the 1950s, however, Eni was considerably smaller than the world's leading multinational oil companies – the so-called "seven sisters" – but Eni's founder, Enrico Mattei was an innovative manager and was able to open up oil imports from the Soviet Union and to create joint ventures with oil producing Middle Eastern countries. When he died in 1963 he left a well-functioning company that continued to be active on a global level with good economic results overall.[35] Eni's petrochemical division was less successful, but this story, which forms part of the woes of the Italian chemical industry in the early 1990s, did not impair its profitability. Eni became a holding entity for a large number of companies, becoming a joint-stock company in 1992 and later privatized, however 26 per cent of its capital is still in the hands of the state-owned bank, CDP, and 4 per cent is held by the Italian ministry of economy and finance.

Enel (Ente nazionale per l'energia elettrica) became in 1963 the state monopoly in the production and distribution of electricity. When it began, Italy was still consuming most of its electricity (80%) from hydro sources, due to its lack of coal and oil.[36] Hydroelectricity had been the Italian brand of energy technology, in which Italian engineers excelled and it is still today the largest component of the renewable energy part of Italian electricity supply. But by the 1950s the exploitation of sites that could be used for dams was complete and it was Enel that was tasked with building thermoelectrical plants. In 1970 oil had become the primary source of electricity (49%) which prompted Enel to diversify its inputs with nuclear plants, especially given Italy's advanced technology in the field. In 1987, however, a national referendum turned down the possibility of using this source[37] and forced Enel to turn to natural gas, which has, today, all but substituted oil in the production of thermoelectricity (coal has always accounted for a very marginal fraction). Since 2007, photovoltaic and wind plants have diminished the use of natural gas, with renewable energy sources reaching 38 per cent of total electricity production in 2016 – above the EU average of 27.5 per cent.[38] While imports, mostly from neighbouring countries, Switzerland and France (which use nuclear plants)[39] are mostly undertaken at night for their low cost, and now account for 10–15 per cent of total supply. Enel was turned into a joint-stock company in 1992 and then privatized, quite effectively, with still today a 23.6 per cent stake in its capital held by the ministry of economy and finance. It has succeeded in internationalizing, acquiring among others control of the Spanish Endesa company and, with 70,000 employees, reaching a size comparable to the French company EdF. It has been the most complex and, arguably, most satisfactory single privatization.

Italian SOEs have included inside their groups important plant design and implementation companies, which, together with some private ones, have put Italy at the forefront of the world market in "specialized engineering firms" which build industrial plants (particularly petrochemical).[40] A final word on the railways. Ferrovie dello Stato (FS), which manages the Italian rail network, is still fully owned by the Italian state. In recent years, its management has greatly improved, building up its programme of high-speed trains (about 1,000 kilometres of line are in operation today and others are being built) and it can boast, in 2016, one of the best budgets in Europe in terms of returns (€9 billion of revenues and 70,000 employees). Plans to privatize it are under consideration.

How should we assess these privatizations? Although launched in 1992, they only began to contribute revenues to the state in 1994. It can be seen from Table 4.7 that the peak period of privatization was reached in the years 1996–99 when Romano Prodi and the following government tried to persuade the EU that Italian public debt could be cut (see Chapter 3) and in the period 2003–05, when Giulio Tremonti, Berlusconi's minister of finances, wanted to step up the process once more. This was precisely the period in which Italian public debt declined as a percentage of GDP (see Figure 3.2). The totals included, in addition, the privatization of public banks, which we shall discuss in a later section. During the financial crisis, new privatizations were few, and the debate continues today whether to continue with privatization or not, with those arguing for the need to cut public debt on one side, against those who argue for the importance of preserving under state control the few big businesses the country has, on the other.

On the whole, most privatizations have been successful, and only smaller enterprises have ended up in foreign hands, but there have been a few high-profile failures as we've seen, notably, steel, telecommunications and airlines.[41] It should be noted that some significant private companies have also run into trouble. We have already mentioned the disappearance of the Italian chemical champion Montedison in the early 1990s, resulting from mistaken government policies and ill-devised managerial strategies, but more often a sale to a foreign buyer results from an unpreparedness to support further growth, as was the case in 2016 when the country's largest cement company, Italcementi[42] was sold to the German company Heidelberg Cement; or when Pirelli (producing tyres since 1872) sold in 2015 to the Chinese company ChemChina. It's also worth noting that the Italian state, through the ministry of economy and finance, and the state-owned bank CDP, still has a substantial presence in the largest of the former SOEs.

Table 4.7 Net revenues from privatizations, 1994–2010 (million euros)

Year	Revenues	Year	Revenues
1994	3,123	2001	2,863
1995	4,018	2002	1,524
1996	6,340	2003	15,540
1997	19,168	2004	8,567
1998	9,951	2005	4,051
1999	18,286	2006–10	683
2000	581	TOTAL	95,168

Source: Ministry of the economy and finance, 2012

At this point, one might very well conclude that Italians are risk averse when it comes to big business, which only the state can manage. This certainly derives, in part, from Italian culture, which is embedded in the high-quality crafts tradition of the past that combines passion for the individual, personalized, expertly-designed product with a willingness to maintain a workplace as "human" and friendly. But it is also the product of the long cultural hegemony of the communist party, which privileged state corporations, and of the DC, which favoured family business. So it was that Italian entrepreneurs developed skills in managing SMEs, but not in managing big business. This has produced a dualism that is now very difficult to overcome.

Table 4.8 Number of companies listed on Italian stock exchange, 1951–2016

	Total	of which AIM Italia
1951	130	
1961	140	
1971	132	
1981	177	
1991	272	
2001	294	
2011	328	10
2016	387	77

Source: Borsa italiana, *Statistiche storiche*

Given this situation, it should come as no surprise that the Italian stock exchange has remained incredibly small (see Table 4.8). Listings did not increase until the late 1980s, so that a doubling of the original 1951 number (130) was only achieved in 1987 (260). The period of privatizations did not make much of an impact (in 2005 the number was 282), and only efforts to allow an easier quotation of SMEs (through AIM Italia, which started in 2009) accounts for the growth to 387 quoted companies in 2016. However, capitalization of the domestic companies quoted, which was €734 billion in 2007, had fallen to €522 billion in 2016 as a result of the financial crisis. The Italian stock exchange was privatized in 1998 and merged with the London Stock Exchange group in 2007.

COOPERATIVE AND SOCIAL ENTERPRISES

In Italy the cooperative form of enterprise has a significant presence. Cooperatives are firms created by its members, people who provide the capital in equal shares and who run the firm on the basis of one member one vote. Typically profits are distributed in accordance with the activity members do within the company – work in workers' cooperatives, purchase in consumer cooperatives, amount of crops conferred in farmers' cooperatives, etc – rather than according to the capital they advance, which only gets a remuneration as a factor of production. Cooperatives have been recognized in the Italian constitution since 1948,[43] where Article 45 states (my translation):

The Republic recognizes the social function of cooperation with a mutual and non-private profit character. The law promotes and supports its diffusion with suitable means and guarantees and ensures with the appropriate controls that its aims are fulfilled.

Cooperatives were first founded in Italy in the nineteenth century, following similar trends in most other European countries; they were persecuted, but not extinguished, by fascism and then flourished after the Second World War, in tune with the traditional Italian disposition favourable to small business and collaborative working practices. They were organized not under one umbrella organization, but under three, according to different ideological backgrounds: the two largest were Legacoop, of socialist-communist inspiration, and Confcooperative, of Catholic inspiration; the third, AGCI (Associazione Generale delle Cooperative Italiane) was constituted only in 1952, but drew on a tradition inspired by the liberal Risorgimento. In 2011 the three organizations embarked on a process of unification to create the ACI (Alleanza Cooperativa Italiana), recognizing that their ideological differences no longer mattered as they had in the past when each of the umbrella organizations had different political parties behind them, and recognizing the need for a strong common organization. This process is still under way at the time of writing.

Thousands of small cooperatives were born in the years of the economic miracle, but their consolidation took place from the 1970s onwards, with an increasing share of employment, rising from 2 per cent to 7 per cent of total employment in 2011.[44] Today, the movement accounts for more than 40,000 companies[45] with 1.3 million employees, 12.5 million members and some €160 billion of revenues. Its importance is far greater in the sectors where it is mostly concentrated (retail and wholesale distribution, finance, agro-industry, catering, transport and logistics, social services) and in those regions where the most important cooperatives have their headquarters (Emilia-Romagna, Trentino). If we add to the cooperative sector, not-for profit enterprises, with almost 1 million employees in 2011, we find that more than 10 per cent of the Italian workers offer their services in the "social economy", a percentage on a par with Belgium and the Netherlands and only slightly below Sweden (11%), with the difference, however, that in Italy cooperatives form the larger component of the total (two-thirds), while in the other countries mentioned it is the opposite.

A brief illustration of the most well-known cooperative achievements will serve to recognize their importance. In agriculture, one third of production (but 60% in the North) is organized through cooperatives, which either distribute produce to the consumers (often through consumer cooperatives) or manage large processing plants in such sectors as dairy, wine (60% of Italian wine is produced in cooperative plants), meat, fruits and vegetables and olive oil. Agricola Tre Valli (meat), Conserve Italia (fruits and vegetables processing), Granarolo (dairies), Orogel (frozen food), Melinda (fruits), Cantine Riunite (wine), Coprob (the only remaining sugar producer in Italy), Consorzio Granterre-Parmareggio (parmesan cheese) are all large food cooperatives. Large retail distribution is dominated by two cooperatives, Coop and Conad, the first a consumer cooperative, the second a retailers' cooperative, which together account for 30 per cent of retail distribution. Both were born out of networks of thousands of smallish cooperatives, which merged and integrated into two tight networks, each with a wholesaler. They dominate the supermarkets and hypermarkets and offer Italian consumers campaigns based on low prices, but also on food safety, support of local traditions, environmental credentials, fair treatment of the labour force, the promotion of cooperation in third world countries, and so on. I might also mention that the largest Italian catering firm is a cooperative, CAMST, based in Bologna,[46] while in Emilia-Romagna Coop and Conad have a two-thirds market share.

Taxi, limousine and coach services all have a significant proportion of cooperatives (25% of employment), mostly in the form of consortia which grant common services to single drivers owing his/her own means of transport. Similarly, facility management is another sector with a high percentage of cooperatives, alongside the allied construction industry, which has been the only cooperative sector to suffer a major reduction in employment, and some notable bankruptcies, since the financial crisis. In the financial sector, Italy has a tight network of smallish credit unions (8% of the market) widely rooted in the smaller Italian municipalities and, as mentioned above, the second largest insurance company in Italy, plus a few other smaller mutual insurance operations. Italy has experienced problems with its popular banks, which do not operate under Article 45 regulating cooperative enterprises and occupy a hybrid position. Some of these banks became very large and went public, others have demutualized and merged with commercial banks. In 2015 the Italian government decided that all popular banks with assets exceeding €8 billion had to demutualize, leaving the other popular banks in their hybrid situation (with some 15% share of the market).

Final mention should go to social cooperatives, also called community cooperatives, which provide social assistance and educational services, including the integration of disadvantaged people into work activities. First appearing in the 1960s, this special type of cooperative is now regulated, under 1991 legislation, and commands half of the Italian market for personal services, employs 400,000 workers and enjoys special fiscal provisions. Local authorities have outsourced to them most of the social services they finance, with high levels of satisfaction on the part of citizens, because social cooperatives in general deliver services at lower costs and at higher quality and try to be innovative in the design of services.

The success of cooperatives in Italy has not only been built on the underlying favourable disposition of Italians towards cooperation, but also because of the extensive networks built by cooperatives, which have sought to substitute network economies for economies of scale, and the legislation that has enabled the capitalization of cooperatives. This legislation consisted of several instruments, the most important of which was allowing cooperatives to acquire loans (and not only share capital) from their members to be invested in the cooperative; consolidating share capital in "indivisible" reserves that cannot be redistributed, without paying corporate tax; and allowing cooperatives to control joint-stock companies with which to form groups. It is ironic that, in relative terms, cooperatives have become larger companies than many private enterprises, but this is primarily explained by their social character, which is valued positively by Italians. Indeed, in 2016 Italy was ready to adopt in its legislation so-called "Bcorp" joint-stock companies which explicitly include social aims in their constitutions.

It is also worth mentioning that in 2016 the "third sector", comprising non-profit enterprises together with foundations and associations, were the subject of a new bill, the aim of which is to promote social entrepreneurship beyond what is already in place. The new bill does not impose on social enterprises any specific legal form, provided that their social mission is made clear in a compulsory "social report", such that the largest part of their profits should be reinvested in the company and their operational management contributes to the generation of community ties where the enterprises are located. To facilitate the promotion of social innovation, new financial instruments are made available to these social enterprises, such as social impact bonds, crowdfunding and, introduced in 2006, the donation on the part of taxpayers of 0.5 per cent of their taxes to specific third sector groups.

THE BANKING SYSTEM

The Italian economy remained a "bank oriented" system after the 1936 banking legislation, but short-term and long-term banking activities were kept apart until the new banking legislation of 1990–93. Short-term lending was provided by savings banks, popular banks, credit unions, and also joint-stock banks, most of which were under IRI, or had their capital in the hands of public institutions. When we add to this the fact that all long-term banks were SOEs, we can say that as much as 80 per cent of the Italian banking sector was either public or cooperative. In 1946 there were 1,378 Italian banks with 7,200 branches; by 1988, there were still as many as 1,100 banks but branches had doubled to 15,447.[47] By then, banks had grown larger, and Italy had 8 of the 100 largest European banks (as against 10 for France, 11 for West Germany and 5 for Britain), but nothing much else had changed and concentration remained low. The only aspect worthy of comment is the peculiarity of Italian long-term credit institutes.

We saw in Chapter 1 the creation of IMI in 1931 in connection with the major bail-out of companies and banks after the 1929 crisis. IMI, based in Rome, became a very large credit institution, to which the DC government of De Gasperi entrusted the administration of all the investment projects carried out in Italy with Marshall Plan funds (1949–52). IMI was innovative in terms of its financing of Italian exports, of new investments in the South, and of applied technological innovation, mostly through financing SOEs. It was also the first credit institution to introduce to Italy investment funds in the 1980s. It merged in 1998 with San Paolo of Turin (Sanpaolo-IMI), and was later brought together with other banks inside a larger group Intesa-Sanpaolo (see below).[48] But IMI was part of a history that included a long list of other investment banks – called collectively ICS (Istituti di credito speciale)[49] – of which the most important was Mediobanca.

Mediobanca was formed in 1946 in Milan, with capital coming from the three IRI banks (Comit, Credit, Banco di Roma), which had once been universal banks, but which could no longer finance long-term investments after the 1936 banking bill. Mediobanca became the bank of Italian private big business, assisting in their survival, consolidation and internationalization, with partial success.[50] Mediobanca has been the only ICS bank to survive the difficulties of the 1990s and remain in business as one of the country's largest banks (see below). It was administered from its foundation until 1982 by Enrico Cuccia (1907–2000), who continued to remain influential in the bank until his death. He was in contact with French, German and US investment banks and was by 1988 able to privatize the bank. The many other ICS institutions were typically connected to groups of commercial banks and ended up being merged with some of them. As a group, the ICS provided the necessary funds for the economic miracle and the support to government policies of "soft" loans to the South and other areas/sectors. For this reason, most (with the exception of Mediobanca) had to face considerable challenges to their budgets arising from the slowdown of the Italian economy in the 1970s and 1980s, with some requiring bailing out.[51]

It was in the watershed years 1990–93 that new legislation – known as the "Amato laws" – comprehensively reformed the Italian banking system. Firstly, it ended the separation between short-term and long-term banking, paving the way to mergers between ICS and commercial banks (as in the case of Sanpaolo-IMI) which resurrected universal banking in Italy. Secondly, it removed the non-profit character of Italian saving banks. By splitting them into two parts, their capital, accumulated over decades, was placed in foundations, which although they maintained the name of the original credit institution, were mandated to sell the bank (incorporated as a joint-stock company fully owned by its foundation) in the market and diversify its investments. Foundations continued the social mission of the former non-profit saving banks, while the banks themselves were managed according to the prevailing capitalist approach, either standing alone or inside groups. Thirdly, the banking reform liberalized the activity of the credit unions, which could enlarge, although nothing was done regarding the popular banks. Finally, it began the process of privatization of IRI banks and others, with the formation of larger banks and banking groups.

Italy has not been a country where philanthropic foundations have mattered much – the small size of companies and the lack of very rich entrepreneurs have discouraged the creation of company foundations – so this was the first time that substantial foundations appeared in Italy, however their size and geographical distribution was not the result of any government decision, but simply mirrored the presence of saving banks in the territory. The number of new foundations constituted was 88, with the North hosting 47, the centre 30 and with only 11 in the South. They have mostly contributed to the preservation of Italy's artistic heritage and the promotion of social activities, particularly in the years before the financial crisis. In fact, although most of the foundations diversified their investments out of their originating bank, they scarcely ventured out of the banking sector, which after the crisis had produced much lower returns and sometimes even loss of capital, as we shall see further.

After the Amato laws, there was a dramatic change in banking. Almost all the great banks in the South failed to convert into private banks and were acquired by northern ones;[52] banks rushed to increase their branches, even beyond their historical locations, while mergers proliferated. In 2000, the number of banks had fallen to 841 (25% less than in 1988), but branches had increased to 27,829 (80% more), to reach a peak of 34,036 in 2009, when banks numbered 788. Among these, only a few banks stood out for size (the two already mentioned, Unicredit and Intesa-Sanpaolo, constituted by countless mergers), and there were some acquisitions by foreign banks. At the time of writing mergers and acquisitions continue. In 2003 the CDP – a state institution since 1863 – was transformed into a joint-stock company under the control of the ministry of economy and finance, and so became the strategic fund for the Italian state and the third largest Italian bank (after the above mentioned two). In 2016 the number of banks had declined to 604 (of which 317 are small credit unions) and branches to 29,027, with a widespread expectation of further cuts to branches and banks.

For the most part Italian banks escaped the financial crisis, having not participated in the derivatives bubble,[53] and did not need bailing out by the state at a time when the governments of most major countries were spending hundreds of billions in such interventions. Although Italy was able to avoid the great increase in public debt that many other countries generated as a result of these bailing-out costs, what was not anticipated was the development of the Italian crisis after 2011, which put so many Italian banks in difficulty as a result of widespread failures of SMEs to which they had given credit. Italian banks therefore accumulated a very large amount of non-performing loans (NPLs),[54] which depressed their profitability and jeopardized their ability to offer further loans, in a few cases bringing banks to insolvency. It was precisely at this point that European banking union came into effect and by January 2016 it obliged members of the Eurozone, through the "single resolution mechanism", not to further bail-out their banks, but instead to use the "bail in" mechanism, namely to hold shareholders and other capital owners and clients of the banks, rather than the state, responsible for the banks difficulties.[55]

It was the first time in Italy that such an approach had been taken, and there followed widespread protests with people believing they were being defrauded of their money invested in banks. Much of 2016 was spent in trying to find ways of dealing with this new emergency. In the end, the following measures were devised: state guarantee for the securitization of NPLs, to be outsourced from banks; reform of credit unions, which would tighten up their small banks in one or two groups; demutualization of the largest popular banks (as mentioned above); and legislation that would speed up the selling of collaterals. In addition, funds collected by banks themselves (and not by the state) were allowed to be used in the capitalization of banks and in refunding some of the smaller shareholders who had lost their money. Mergers and acquisitions continue to take place in this context. At the time of writing, Italy has around 100 banking groups and the general situation of its banking system has improved, making the participation of Italy in the European banking union a point of fact.

TOURISM

Italian "tourism" has a very ancient origin, dating back to Rome's thermal resorts as a destination for the rich and the cultivated people of its empire. With the spreading of Christianity, Rome became – and still is – the destination for many pilgrimages, while other Italian places on the route of pilgrimages, mostly to Jerusalem and Santiago de Compostela (Spain), also became destinations, especially for the worship of saints and the Virgin Mary. Among the most famous Italian locations, Padua (St Anthony), Loreto (the house of the holy family) and Assisi (St Francis) stand out, but there are thousands of famous basilicas, churches and monasteries across the country. And at the time of the grand tour (see Chapter 1), Italy attracted the youth of Europe's wealthy elites to attend universities, art and music schools and to admire the architecture and visual culture of the many Italian cities.

While modern tourism was born in England in the first half of the nineteenth century, Italy was quick to develop it, taking advantage of the diversity of the Italian landscape, from the high mountains of the Alps, to the beautiful hills of the Apennines, from the northern lakes, to the long scenic coastlines. What makes Italy particularly attractive to tourism is that it has retained an incredibly high number of its medieval-Renaissance towns and cities, most of which have very well preserved city centres. Some of these cities are unique in the world – Venice with its canals, Florence with its Renaissance churches and palaces, and of course Rome and its Roman architecture – but numerous smaller cities are jewels of medieval, renaissance and baroque architecture, while hundreds of museums display 3,000 years of the country's artefacts. Italy boasts 54 UNESCO world heritage sites, more than China (50), most of which are architectural sites, such as the city of Matera, with its houses carved into the stone hills; the houses of Alberobello (Puglia), of circular construction with a conical straw roof; the baroque palaces of Noto (Sicily); the medieval tower mansions of San Gemignano (Tuscany); and the old fishing villages of the Cinque Terre (Liguria). The geographical distribution of villas with Italian-style gardens, frescoed palaces, castles, fountains and arcades throughout the country make the touring of Italy a continuous surprise, especially when itineraries include the numerous culinary and wine traditions of the country, and the many locally-produced craft and artisan products.[56]

For these reasons, the Italian tourist sector is diffuse and for the most part operates from small premises, or historical hotels, not so suited to mass tourism, although major mountain and sea resorts have built more modern hotels, but typically non-standardized, often family managed and with limited capacity. Many Italians possess second homes (15% of families) in the country or by the sea, many inherited from parents, or bought for weekends and holidays. All this has made tourism one of the country's major industries. In the international tourism stakes, Italy is fifth after France[57], the United States, China and Spain, but when taking into account that a large majority of Italians spend their holidays in Italy, VA directly produced by the tourism industry is 6 per cent of total GDP, slightly below Spain (6.5%), but above France (4%), the UK (3.8%) and Germany (3.2%).[58] If we add the indirect multiplier, the tourism industry is estimated at 10 per cent of Italian GDP employing 2.6 million people (11.6%), one third of it in cultural tourism.[59] It is worth noting also that tourism has always contributed to Italy's balance of payments because revenues in this sector have always exceeded expenditure and because Italy offers congenial environments for international business and cultural meetings, with the help of the various exhibition spaces that it hosts.

The recent development of agro-tourism and services, like Airbnb, have enabled the Italian tourism industry to fill its disparate capacity, making better use of second houses, or partly used ones. What has been missing from the sector, until recently, is a capacity to be innovative in the use of digital platforms, although it is now possible to book accommodation almost anywhere in Italy from one's personal computer. Also, it's worth mentioning the services offered to visitors besides food and shelter: excursions to museums, boat/train trips, bicycle drives, eco-gastronomic tours, etc. As in many other fields, Italy cannot compete in terms of standardized quantity, but it does excel in the quality, diversity and customization of services.[60] In 2014, the Fondazione Italia Patria della Bellezza was established to promote the cultural heritage of the country. Research financed by the foundation and published in 2017[61] fixes at €240 billion in 2013 (16.5% of GDP) the VA of activities concerned with culture (products, creative technologies and design, tourism, public investments in cultural infrastructures, cultural philanthropy). More could still be done to promote the cultural component of Italian GDP, given the vast and still relatively unexploited cultural wealth of the country.

5

Human factors

We have already seen in Chapter 3 the basic demographic indicators for the country: a long life-expectancy, a very low fertility rate, an unsatisfactory rate of women employment and substantial immigration. In this chapter I will focus first on the family, beginning with its strong traditional role, before examining its changed composition, how it has fared in the face of economic crisis, and the position of women. I will then consider education and human capital, before discussing the issue of immigration, with special attention given to the recent migrant crisis and the resumption of Italian emigration abroad.

FAMILY, AGE AND GENDER

Italy has shared the "nuclear" form of the family since the Middle Ages, with a propensity to retain very strong family ties. These ties can tend towards nepotism and even to amoral familism,[1] however, in its positive version family ties have guaranteed a network of support and friendship that has lasted to this very day, although the situation of the Italian family is today very different with 58 per cent of "households" comprising one or two people and only 6 per cent having more than four members.

Over a third of households have a family head over 65 years of age. When we take into account that Italy has 3 million seriously disabled people (2.2 million over 65 years of age) and only 2 million receive state assistance, and only 22 per cent of children under the age of three attend preschool, it is easy to understand that the majority of families are engaged in the care of children and old people. Some resort to private help, although there is no clear information about the size of that help. In 2016 the Italian National Agency for Pension Schemes (INPS) reported 900,000 people enrolled as home helpers whose social contributions are paid by families, but it is well-known that there are an additional 600,000 "badanti" (caregivers to old people in their houses), mostly Eastern European migrants, who do not have an official contract of employment, plus an unknown number of child-minders who look after small children when parents are at work.

The impact of aging is a matter of great concern in Italy because of its spill-over effects in many areas: the increase in health-care expenditures, in social assistance and the payment of pensions, in spite of the major reforms enacted; the increase in the burden of old people on the working population; the negative impact on the rate of entrepreneurship and innovation coming from a shrinking class of young people; and the increasing risk averse approach of the population to the use of savings. As a partial counterbalancing effect, there is a tendency today for old people to remain more active than in the past, both as a result of the new pension regulations that have lengthened the working life, but also because an increasing share of the older generation wish to remain active.[2]

As far as family legislation is concerned, in 1975 there was a major reform of family law, in which parity of rights inside the family was achieved, while divorce was introduced in law in 1970 and abortion in 1978, as we mentioned in Chapter 2. Further legislation regarding families followed: in 2012 legislation lifted all discrimination between children born to married couples and those born outside marriage (28% of newly born children in 2014); in 2015 legislation made divorce easier, shortening the length of time between separation and divorce to 6–12 months; and in 2016 both same sex couples and unmarried couples were given most of the legal protections afforded to married couples. These later measures came as a consequence of the diversification Italian families had experienced, in particular the increasing impact of divorce. In 1990, the divorce rate in Italy stood at 0.5 per 1000 (or 5 per 10,000) inhabitants, slowly increasing to 0.9 per 1000 (or 9 per 10,000) in 2014, when it was still one of the lowest in Europe. When the 2015 legislation was enacted, and thus shortening the process from separation to divorce, the divorce rate rose to 1.4 per 1,000 (or 14 per 10,000) inhabitants, still among the lowest in Europe, but not so markedly lower as before. Italian families have also seen an increasing number of unmarried couples, of couples not married in church, of remarried couples and of same sex couples.

Other features of the Italian family worth noting are as follows. Although young people typically marry in Italy in their 30s, as in most other European countries, they tend to remain with their family until they marry, a pattern shared only with other Mediterranean countries. So, in the 30–34 age group, 40 per cent of men and 25 per cent of women are still living with their parents, due in part to the impact of the financial crisis on young people's employment. Much research has been published that criticizes this trend, speaking of "bamboccioni" ("mummy's boys") who grow up incapable of taking up responsibility for home management.

This brings me to a discussion of the position of women in Italy. It must be made clear that from a *legislative* point of view, there is no discrimination against women in pay or conditions of work (parity was introduced in 1977) and the wage gap at low and intermediate levels is small (6%, due mostly to less overtime taken by women). The real problem is that Italian women reach the very top positions more seldom than men. This is mostly due to the organization of the family, where it remains the case that most of the domestic activities and childcare duties are the responsibility of women, which discourages female employment and taking on jobs with greater demands and burdens.[3]

In recent years, there have been efforts to encourage greater harmonization between work and family life, especially on the part of the more far-sighted companies.[4] "Smart work", part-time positions, a variety of services offered to employees to cut childcare costs and cover the shortage of time to accomplish domestic duties[5] have constituted an increasing part of the additional benefits negotiated between trade unions and employers at company level. This development now involves more than 50 per cent of Italian companies and is known as "second welfare" or "company's welfare".[6] In-house training is also made available to strengthen women's career opportunities and help them break the glass ceiling. In 2011 legislation imposed a legal requirement that a third of Board directors of quoted and state-owned companies must be women. In 2016 the share of women directors had reached 31 per cent, which althouth the fourth highest in Europe (after Norway, France and Sweden), still suggests that it is more a problem of public attitudes rather than legislation that is still retarding the position of women in Italian society.

During the financial crisis, the Italian family has shown its resilience, helping its younger members, many without jobs, by housing them at home, or financing their accommodation, providing childcare, or trying to find them a job. It is a paradox of contemporary life that in many cases the pensions of the old are the source of survival for the younger generation, with intergenerational transfers being the reverse of those in the past. The Italian economy's poor labour market conditions of the past twenty years have created a desperate situation for those in their twenties and thirties, providing only precarious jobs with low pay, and discontinuing the social mobility that previous generations enjoyed. Today only a small fraction of young working people receive an income higher than that of their parents; and family ties have played a major role in softening the impact of this.[7] Parents and grandparents are able do this because they have accumulated remarkable wealth in the past, given that Italian's propensity to save has always been quite high.

A comparative analysis of the level of wealth per adult in 2016 is reported in Table 5.1. There is much to be learnt from the data in this table. There was a significant increase in wealth in all the countries included; only Greece and Japan had lower growth rates. The figures for the United States and the Netherlands present a very high level of financial wealth, while Greece's represents the lowest (for understandable reasons). Italy,

Table 5.1 Wealth per adult in selected countries, 2000 and 2016 (current $ at market exchange rates)

	2000	2016	% financial assets 2016	% debts 2016	Share of total wealth of top 1%
	1	2	3	4	5
Canada	108,464	270,179	53	17	26
France	103,619	244,365	39	12	25
Germany	89,770	185,175	41	13	31
Greece	73,920	103,569	22	13	24
Japan	191,877	230,946	60	14	18
South Korea	51,749	159,914	37	17	28
Netherlands	106,872	184,378	70	29	24
Portugal	48,008	77,113	48	21	28
Spain	64,521	116,320	41	16	27
Sweden	73,046	227,295	62	21	36
UK	162,999	288,808	52	14	24
USA	206,116	344,692	72	14	42
Italy	**119,773**	**202,288**	**39**	**9**	**25**

Source: Credit Suisse Global Wealth Databook, 2016

France, Spain, Germany and South Korea show a quite moderate level, which indicates a more direct investment by families in property. It needs to be noted that the wealth reported by Credit Suisse is gross and must be netted of debts, reported in column 4. It can clearly be seen that Italian families try to avoid debt, which only forms 9 per cent of their wealth. Finally, the last column reports the share of total wealth in the hands of the richest 1 per cent of the population. While Japan stands out with the lowest percentage, the European countries are very similar in their performance, with the exception of Sweden and to a lesser extent Germany.[8] The difference with the United States is startling, but the countries showing the most pronounced concentration of wealth in the hands of the top 1 per cent are Russia (74%) and the most prominent developing countries (Brazil 48%, China 44%, India 58%, Indonesia 49%, and Thailand 58%). The real wealth of Italian families and its wide distribution across the population is a major factor in explaining the resilience of the country in the face of the worst economic crisis the country has faced in its 115 years of unification (other than the years of the two world wars).

EDUCATION AND RESEARCH

After the Second World War, illiteracy had yet to be defeated in the centre and south of the country, particularly in the latter, where, in 1951, illiteracy rates were still around 25 per cent. This is a long story, dating back to the worst of the legacies of Bourbon control of southern Italy before unification, and its total lack of interest in education provision.[9] By 1981 the situation had improved (although illiteracy remained a feature within the older generation), with enrolment rates (calculated as the number of students enrolled as a percentage of the youngsters of the relevant age) in secondary schools and universities having increased, the former from 11 per cent in 1951 to 52 per cent in 1981, the latter from 3.5 per cent to 17 per cent. Since then, enrolment rates have continued to improve for secondary schools, attaining a level of around 80 per cent, which is a little on the low side when compared to other OECD countries, but the same as the United States. However, the trend has not been as positive for higher education, for which Italy has a rate of enrolment – and especially a level of attainment – which is among the lowest of OECD countries. Using the official data from Eurostat and OECD, in 2014, 42 per cent of the Italian population aged between 15 and 64 had reached a level of education equivalent to lower secondary education, 12 per cent above the EU average and 43 per cent had reached a level equivalent to upper secondary education, more or less the EU average. However, those reaching the level of tertiary education amounted to only 15 per cent, 11 per cent below the EU average and well below the UK (37%), France (30%), Sweden (33%), the Netherlands (30%) and Spain (32%). The situation is improving, but gaps remain. Data in 2016 relating to the percentage of people aged 30–34 with a tertiary degree, show Italy at 26 per cent (with France at 44%, Spain 40%, the Netherlands 46%, the UK 48%, Sweden 43%, and Germany at 33%). In line with other advanced countries, the percentage of women attending university and getting a degree in Italy is much higher than for men.

Why this striking Italian anomaly in rates of higher education? It is generally argued that one of the chief reasons is the way Italian universities are organized. Indeed, until the 1970s universities were elite institutions, but after having opened up to mass enrolment, concerted efforts have been made to help students from all backgrounds get a degree. Dropout rates of enrolled students have gone down over time, but today still about one third of enrolled university students do not get a degree. In reality, however, the problem stems not so much from the supply side but from the demand side. What is observed is that, while by international standards universities in Italy graduate too few people, by national standards they graduate too many, something illustrated by the high level of Italian graduates going abroad to find work, as we shall see in the next section. Italy's sectors of specialization and the small size of its businesses has given rise to a labour market with a very low level of demand for young people with a tertiary degree. Many Italian jobs are learned through on the job training and secondary education is sufficient to manage small firms. This is true not only for the fashion industry, which rewards creativity and practical experience rather than formal education, but is also true for engineering, where there is significant training on the job after technical or vocational secondary school – something that also applies to Germany and which explains why Germany also has lower levels of tertiary education.

An aside about Italy's North–South divide. A recent piece of research has offered a regional analysis of Human Development Index (HDI) for the Italian regions over the period, 1871–2007. HDI was proposed by the UN in 1990 as an indicator that would go beyond per capita GDP in regional and international comparisons. It is an average of three indicators, normalized to vary from 0 to 1: life expectancy, education (literacy rate and gross enrolment ratio) and per capita income, compounded through a geometric mean.[10] Relevant results are shown in Table 5.2, where the convergence of the three indicators 1951–2007 is reported separately, together with the final HDI (called hybrid because of some specific adjustments made by the authors). What we can note is that convergence with other countries on life expectancy has easily been reached (something already shown in Chapter 3); convergence of the educational indicator, remarkably divergent in 1951 has also been achieved, but convergence of per capita GDP is still lagging behind. The result is that the HDI does not signal the same profound difference between North and South as per capita GDP alone. The authors of this work speak of "passive modernization", meaning that what could be done by the state (a welfare system to improve health, schooling to improve education) has been done, but that this was not sufficient to produce a complete convergence of economic performance of the regions. We can certainly argue that things would be much worse if life expectancy and education had not converged, but what is certain is that HDI as an indicator does not help much in understanding Italian dualism.[11] Social capital might be more relevant to explain the North–South divide, a topic we will examine in Chapter 6.

The distribution of university students across subjects is diverse, with a significant concentration in law, literature, languages and teaching (see Table 5.3). In 2006 an agency (ANVUR) tasked with the evaluation of university performance was created, which has, at the time of writing,

Table 5.2 Hybrid HDI by region, 1951–2007

	Longevity Italy = 1		Education Italy = 1		Per capita GDP Italy = 1		Hybrid HDI	
	1951	2007	1951	2007	1951	2007	1951	2007
North-West	1.00	1.00	1.09	1.00	1.49	1.13	0.67	0.90
North-East	1.04	1.01	1.04	1.00	1.11	1.17	0.65	0.91
Centre	1.04	1.01	1.03	1.04	0.91	1.04	0.64	0.91
South	0.95	0.99	0.88	0.98	0.68	0.78	0.57	0.88
Islands	0.97	0.99	0.91	0.99	0.59	0.78	0.57	0.88
ITALY	1.00	1.00	1.00	1.00	1.00	1.00	0.63	0.90

Source: Felice & Vasta 2015

Table 5.3 University students by subject, 2015

	%
Science	3.2
Chemistry/Pharmacy	4.1
Biology	4.3
Medicine	10.8
Engineering	13.0
Architecture	4.9
Agriculture	2.8
Economics/Statistics	13.6
Politics/Sociology	9.3
Law	10.5
Literature	7.3
Languages	5.9
Teaching	4.5
Psychology	3.8
Sport	2.0
Other	0.1
TOTAL	100.0

Source: Istat

completed two rounds of evaluation, and revealed what was largely known already, namely that Italian universities, despite almost all being public,[12] ranked quite diversely in terms of performance. According to the latest ranking by ANVUR, which considers separately large, medium-sized and small universities, the universities of Padua, Bologna and Turin achieve the highest number of positions in the 14 research areas identified. The universities of Milan collectively also achieve a high number of top positions, followed by the universities of Rome, Pisa, Florence, Venice and Trento. This explains the high attraction rate of these universities to students from other regions. That the best universities are in the more advanced regions also encourages students, keen to find employment locally when they complete their studies.

Internationally, Italian universities generally rank low, because they have been incapable until very recently of taking part in the wider context of English-speaking higher education. Only recently have some of the better universities started to offer courses in English, attracting for the first time foreign students and foreign professors, while most research outputs today are written in English, especially in science, medicine and economics. Indeed, the impact factor of Italian researchers has improved, reaching a higher level than the EU average, and when taking into account the meagre resources they can avail themselves of, Italian researchers are very productive. The polytechnics (technical universities) of Milan, Turin, Bologna, Bari, Naples and other smaller ones are busy creating start-ups in electronics, new materials, robotics, green chemicals, biopharmaceuticals, nanotechnologies, aerospace, drones, renewable energies, self-driven cars, but also in the restoration of old buildings, paintings and monuments, in a nutshell, Industry 4.0.

The difficulty has been to find sufficient funding to finance these new ideas. In this regard, we have to remind ourselves again that Italy is largely disadvantaged by not having enough big business with their immense research facilities, by having a South that is lagging behind, and a concentration in sectors, such as tourism, in which innovation is very largely peripheral. It is inevitable, therefore, that expenditure in R & D as a percentage of GDP in Italy is very low, less than 1.4 per cent, half public and half private (the average for the EU is 2%). That the problem is connected with the size of firms can be shown by some of Istat's figures: only 40 per cent of firms with 10–49 employees report product and process innovation (and nothing is said of the smaller ones!), whereas 63 per cent innovate in the class of 50–249 employees and 77 per cent in the class over 250. The contribution of regional dualism is also clearly seen: Piemonte and Trento's R & D expenditure reaches 1.9 per cent of GDP, Emilia-Romagna and

Lazio 1.6 per cent, Friuli 1.5 per cent (surprisingly Lombardia is average), while as many as 11 regions are below 1 per cent, 5 of which are below 0.5 per cent. Amongst the bottom ranking in R & D expenditure are the tourist areas of Val d'Aosta, the very last with 0.4 per cent, and Bolzano, with 0.5 per cent. The other mainly tourist area – Trento – is among the highest because it hosts some industry as well and has a high investment in skiing infrastructure. It must also be taken into account that state expenditure in the field of research has been cut as a result of Italian budget difficulties and those companies and universities which are doing well are those that have been able to work as part of European networks of research or which are connected with large transnational corporations. We should also note that many researchers trained in Italy with public money end up in foreign laboratories, European as well as American, often successful, because the average level of education offered by the best Italian universities is quite high. The great loss that this produces for the Italian economy is part of the vicious circle which Italy is today struggling to escape from.

While the Internet and associated new media are quite widespread (75 per cent of companies with more than 10 employees have a website), only 11 per cent of companies transact direct sales online, with half of internet users having shopped online. Two thirds of Italians (aged 6 and over) use the Internet, but the percentage increases to 83 per cent for the age group 11–14, and to 92 per cent for the 15–24 group, with the rate dropping below the average only for the ages above 60. The diffusion of broadband connectivity is not complete, but only remote villages in rural or mountainous areas remain not covered. In 2015 employment in information and communications technology (ICT) reached 3.2 per cent of total employment (as against 3.6% in France and 3.7% in Germany).

MIGRATION

As we have seen in Chapter 2, the years of the economic miracle were years of intense Italian emigration abroad and of intense relocation of the southern Italian population to the North and centre. During the 1970s and

1980s, Italian mobility decreased to very low levels and there it remained until the end of the 1990s. Then the movement of people from the South picked up again, first in connection with the slowing down of the economy and then with the financial crisis, and the trend is expected to continue. Adriano Giannola, the president of SVIMEZ (the research institution devoted to the study of the southern economy) and professor of economics in Naples, sadly writes in one of his essays of a "final solution" to the southern problem: exit.[13] Between the two census years, 2001 and 2011, the South lost half a million people, mostly young, who relocated to the North-centre of the country, a third of them with a university degree.

The resumption of net Italian emigration abroad is instead a more recent phenomenon, partly blurred by the contemporary surge of foreign immigration (to which we will turn later). In the 2016 report of the Migrantes foundation it can be seen that until 2007 net migration of Italians abroad was near zero: movements out were compensated by movements in at a rate of some 40,000 people per year. Between 2008 and 2010, emigration remained more or less at its previous level, while immigration reduced; from 2011 onwards emigration climbed, to the 2015 and 2016 peaks of 107,529 and 115,000 respectively. The gap between Italians going abroad and those coming back (net migration) stands at 80,000, mostly young people, 50 per cent of which are from the South (which has also lost numbers to the North, as we have seen above). These figures are from Istat; the Migrantes foundation instead uses the number of Italians who each year register abroad, suggesting that the Istat numbers should be somewhat increased.

According to the Migrantes foundation, there are 4.9 million Italians with Italian citizenship living abroad, 2.7 million of whom are in Europe (Germany, Switzerland, France, the UK, Belgium) and 1.6 million in Latin America (Argentina, Brazil, Uruguay, Chile). There is a mounting concern in Italy about the increasing loss of Italian human capital. It has been estimated that the creation of such human capital has a per capita cost of €400,000. From this it is easy to reach a total cost of tens of billions of euros of Italian human capital not being employed in the country and adding instead to the human capital of other countries. However, it must be taken into consideration that today mobility, of young people especially, is much greater than in the past and it is reasonable to expect that some of the recent outflows would be reversed if the Italian economy recovers.

Figure 5.1 International mobility of Italian citizens, 2000–15

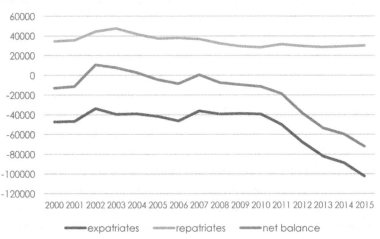

Source: Istat

We are now in a position to examine one of the major economic and political issues facing Italy and Europe in recent years, namely immigration. The net rate of immigration in Italy remained extremely low up until the 1990s, then it grew slowly, peaking with the new millennium until 2007 (with a trough in 2006) and declining with fluctuations over the financial crisis. However, it still remains higher today than in the 1990s, as can be seen in Figure 5.2. This has produced a major change for Italy, which had never previously been a country impacted by immigration, enlarging for the first time in the life of the country its foreign resident population (as Table 5.4 shows for the census years up to 2016). From a negligible share of the population until the 1990s, the foreign resident population has today reached 8.3 per cent. If we include the foreign-born people who hold Italian citizenship, we can add another one million people,[14] reaching a total of around 6 million, 10 per cent of the Italian population. In Table 5.5, it is possible to present a comparison with other European countries, based on this more comprehensive data set that includes national citizens born abroad. As immigration for Italy has only been a recent trend, at 10 per cent, Italy is still comparatively low, but Table 5.5 also shows that as a country it has experienced the most rapid increase over the past 15 years.

Figure 5.2   Rate of net migration, 1990–2016 (on 1000 population)

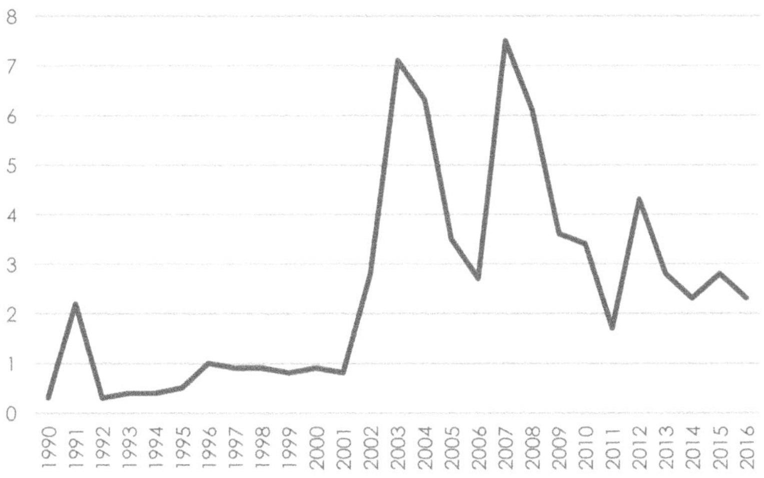

Source: Istat

If we look at the composition of this foreign population, only 30 per cent is from EU countries, with a large predominance of Eastern European migrants. The single largest community is from Romania (23%), followed by Albania (10%) and Morocco (9%). But the presence of migrants from China, the Philippines, Ukraine, India, Bangladesh, Pakistan is also significant; overall Italy hosts migrants from 200 different countries. In terms of gender the overall composition is balanced, but not by nation of origin: for example, the "badanti" (see above) are almost all women and come mostly from Ukraine, Poland, the Philippines, Moldova, Ecuador and other Latin America countries. In 2014 the total volume of migrant remittances – money sent home by migrants living in Italy – exceeded €5 billion. When we consider the regional distribution of Italian immigration we can see that the North-Centre has a share of migrants of around 10.7 per cent (with peaks in Lombardia, 11.5% and Emilia-Romagna, 12%), while the South stands at 3.6 per cent. This would suggest that migrants to Italy were mostly "economic" migrants, attracted to those regions with the highest levels of economic activity. What is important to note is that, due to the highly decentralized nature of Italian business, there are no large concentrations of migrants in one part of the country. Instead they are dispersed throughout small and medium-sized cities, without a tendency to form ghettos, although here and there one can find exceptions.[15] Also, the relative recent settlement of these migrants coming from so many different countries of origin and the readiness of local authorities and non-profit organizations to put in place policies of integration have in general prevented the formation of closed communities. Racist episodes have taken place in Italy, but they are not frequent.

Table 5.4   Foreign residents in Italy, 1961–2016

	No.	% of population
1961	62,780	0.1
1971	121,116	0.2
1981	210,937	0.4
1991	356,159	0.6
2001	1,334,889	2.3
2011	4,027,627	6.8
2016	5,029,000	8.3

Source: Istat

Things, however, have radically changed in recent years, beginning in 2014, when the Mediterranean Sea witnessed the exodus of dislocated people from the Middle East and Sub-Saharan Africa. In 2014, 170,000 migrants crossed over to Italy from North Africa and in the following year, Italy received 153,843 migrants. In 2015, the "Balkan route" through Greece and the Balkan countries had opened up, which saw some 850,000 people enter Europe, with most asking for asylum in Germany. In November 2016 an agreement was reached between the European Union and the Turkish government to shelter and assist refugees from Syria in Turkey (some 3 million), against a EU disbursement of €3 billion for 2016 and 2017 (Refugee Facility for Turkey). EU support to refugee camps also extended to refugees in Lebanon (1 million Syrians, plus half a million from other countries) and Jordan (650,000 Syrians, plus 2.1 million Palestinians). Despite EU initiatives, the flow of migrants to Italy continued, reaching 181,436 in 2016, with most crossing over from Libya and originating in Sub-Saharan countries, with an increasing number of unaccompanied minors. At present, efforts are being made to check this flow, by helping the reorganization of Libya and trying to stem the flows coming to Libya from the Sub-Saharan countries.

This refugee crisis has had three dimensions to it, which we will briefly discuss. Firstly, its impact on EU asylum and migration policy, which has had to be revised as a consequence has caused enormous tension with those EU member states that have refused to collaborate, especially in the relocation of migrants from Greece and Italy. Frontex, the EU institution responsible for the control of EU borders, too has had to be reorganized.[16] At the time of writing, this revision has taken place, but it is not operative yet. However, there is still much to be done at EU level, because the solutions so far proposed (mostly huge refugee camps supported by EU funds) are temporary. Secondly, Italy's response, the Italian government has had to organize the accommodation of all these people reaching its shores, mostly in Sicily. Although first hosted there, it soon became clear that this was unsustainable, and all Italian municipalities were asked to share in hosting the migrants. Thus, they have been spread across the country,

Table 5.5 Foreign-born population by EU country, 2015

	Total		Born in another EU Member State		Born in a non-member country	
	(thousands)	(% of the population)	(thousands)	(% of the population)	(thousands)	(% of the population)
Belgium	1845.6	16.3	866.8	7.7	978.8	8.7
Bulgaria	136.4	1.9	48.5	0.7	87.9	1.2
Czech Republic	433.3	4.1	171.8	1.6	261.5	2.5
Denmark	636.7	11.2	216.9	3.8	419.8	7.4
Germany	10908.3	13.3	4351.8	5.3	6556.4	8.0
Estonia	193.3	14.7	19.2	1.5	174.6	13.3
Ireland	798.6	16.9	547.6	11.6	251.0	5.3
Greece	1220.4	11.3	350.1	3.2	870.3	8.1
Spain	5919.2	12.7	1957.0	4.2	3962.2	8.5
France	7902.6	11.8	2203.8	3.3	5699.0	8.5
Croatia	547.9	13.1	68.6	1.6	479.4	11.4
Italy	5907.5	9.7	1823.8	3.0	4083.6	6.7
Cyprus	172.8	20.4	110.4	13.0	62.4	7.4
Latvia	258.9	13.1	27.6	1.4	231.3	11.7
Lithuania	129.7	4.5	20.8	0.7	108.9	3.8
Luxemburg	260.6	45.2	194.8	33.8	65.8	11.4
Hungary	503.8	5.1	320.5	3.3	183.3	1.9
Malta	45.9	10.6	20.7	4.8	25.1	5.8
Netherlands	2056.5	12.1	554.9	3.3	1501.6	8.8
Austria	1578.2	18.2	713.6	8.2	864.6	9.9
Poland	626.4	1.6	216.3	0.6	410.1	1.1
Portugal	872.5	8.4	232.0	2.2	640.5	6.2
Romania	350.8	1.8	148.4	0.8	202.3	1.0
Slovenia	241.2	11.7	67.0	3.2	174.2	8.4
Slovakia	181.6	3.3	150.5	2.8	31.1	0.6
Finland	329.2	6.0	118.8	2.2	210.4	3.8
Sweden	1675.1	17.0	529.8	5.4	1145.3	1.6
United Kingdom	8698.2	13.3	3250.6	5.0	5447.5	8.3
Iceland	41.9	12.6	28.1	8.5	13.7	4.1
Lichtenstein	24.2	64.4	8.2	21.9	16.0	42.5
Norway	774.0	14.9	349.7	6.7	424.3	8.1
Switzerland	2324.5	27.9	1393.6	16.7	930.9	11.2

Source: Eurostat (online data code: migr_pop3ctb)

Note: the values for the different categories of country of birth may not sum to the totals due to rounding.

avoiding major concentrations in single places (with a few exceptions). Both the local authorities and NGOs have collaborated in providing camps and facilities, although EU funds to support this process have in some instances been misused.

The third major issue concerns the way these migrants have reached their Italian destination. They typically arrive in makeshift boats provided by criminal organizations, traffickers and smugglers, that run the risk of sinking and which rely on being rescued by patrol ships from the Italian navy, Frontex, and vessels financed by charitable organizations. The need to rescue every day thousands of migrants who are in danger of drowning in the waters of the Mediterranean is an alarming and paradoxical situation in the present age. Public opinion often argues that these people would be better helped to remain in their own country, but such a strategy requires a long-term engagement, which entails a very different approach to foreign policy on the part of European member states. We can agree with Jean-Claude Juncker, president of the EU Commission since 2014, that the organization by Italy of countless rescue operations in the Mediterranean Sea has rescued not only tens of thousands of people, but the "honour" of Europe. But it is not enough, and the role Europe plays in Africa must be entirely rethought.

Finally, a more general conclusion on the impact of migration on Italy. Productivity in Italy over the past 15 years has stagnated. This is partly due to lack of investment and the decline of the economy, but in no small part it has also been due to the impact of millions of new workers from outside the country. With so many migrants amassed in such a short span of time, only poor jobs and poorly organized jobs with low wages are available to them. The paradox is that not all of the migrants reaching Italy are poorly educated or unskilled, but rather their jobs often do not adequately exploit their educational background. I have mentioned in Chapter 4 that competitive Italian firms have a level of productivity comparable to their competitors abroad, but it is the rest of the Italian economy, particularly in some services and in construction, where productivity needs to improve, and doing so in no small part by increasing the performance of migrants.

6

Social factors

Social capital presents in Italy quite contrasting features. On one side, the country enjoys one of the lowest rates of homicide, suicide and imprisoned people in the world. We have already observed that the health of its people is among the best in the world, with life expectancy among the highest; moreover, Italy records a low level of alcohol consumption (the lowest in Europe), good and varied food (the famous "Mediterranean diet"), limited obesity, widespread home ownership, many opportunities for socially-based entertainment and leisure time; and a strong network of associations and NGOs. On the other side, the country has a very high level of corruption, high tax evasion and the widespread existence of organized crime. Let us begin with social and civic capital and its measurement.

SOCIAL AND CIVIC CAPITAL

The concepts of "social capital" and "civic virtues" as foundations for the economic flourishing of communities go back to the Italian city-states of the Middle Ages, when economic activity was justified by theologians if it aimed at the "common good" ("*fare ricca la città*" – to enrich the city) and they continued to be elaborated until a much narrower vision of economics prevailed in the nineteenth century in the Anglo-Saxon countries.[1] Since then utilitarianism and self-interest have formed the basis of economic theory, but in Italy economic practice has maintained contact with some of the social roots of that original thinking. The reproposition of social capital as an important determinant of positive economic performance came firstly from the work of sociologists in the 1980s and 1990s (especially Pierre Bourdieu and Robert Putnam).[2] Social capital was defined as the set of factors enabling people to act together effectively in pursuing shared aims and it was based on relationships of trust. There was also an effort to articulate social capital according to its different coverage in society: *bonding*, when trust and common endeavour is limited to family ties; *bridging*, when it is centred on local connections; *linking*, when the extension of connections is unlimited. Bonding social capital, generally, has been viewed negatively, because it can lock groups into sects or clans, and activate conflicts among groups and between groups and the rest of society. Indeed, mafia groups contain bonding social capital, which can hardly be considered valuable social capital. The concept of social capital as it was originally defined remains ambivalent, it can be good or bad for society.

When the idea of social capital spread to a wider range of social science disciplines including economics, the need for a more accurate conceptualization and measurement of it became apparent, to distinguish it clearly from human capital, to give it only a positive connotation and to include it in econometric models. More lately, it has been proposed to define social capital as *civic* capital,[3] identifying it with "those persistent and shared beliefs and values that help a group overcome the free rider problem in the pursuit of socially valuable activities".[4] Defined like this, social capital can be distinguished clearly from human capital, it eschews negative connotations and it becomes a long-run feature of societies transmitted by family and other institutions. It contributes to the production of "social cohesion", together with a more equal distribution of income, lower levels of unemployment and higher levels of human capital. There are historical, geographical and political conditions that favour/disfavour the building up of social/civic capital and its level can be measured by means of surveys (mostly enquiring about trust relations) and experiments or through indirect indicators, such as the propensity to donation (of blood or organs, for example); participation in voluntary activities; voter turnout; the persistence over time of democratic or autocratic regimes; the tendency to violate social norms (tax evasion, bribery, fare-dodging); the number of "networks" of civic engagement (associations, choral societies, music societies, sports clubs, drama groups). The results of the large body of research which has sought to define and measure social capital point invariably to the importance of social capital in determining development, which is found to be more substantial and longer lasting where social capital is higher.

Italian research making use of social capital concepts has mostly gone in the direction of demonstrating the different regional endowment of social capital – higher in the North and lower in the South – as can be shown from Istat's data that underpins its report on "Fair and Sustainable Wellbeing" (BES, *Benessere equo e sostenibile*). The report is based on 130 basic series, summarized in 12 domains: health, education, work, income, social relations, politics and institutions, security, life satisfaction, environment, research and innovation, quality of services. Selecting from the three domains of social relations, politics and institutions, and security, Table 6.1 lists a number of indicators connected with social capital. What comes out of this picture is invariably that all such social indicators are worse in the South, with the centre closer to the North. Within the North, the regions that stand out as best are the two bilingual regions Valle d'Aosta and Trentino Alto Adige, and also Friuli Venezia Giulia. In the centre, Lazio drags down all the indicators, testifying to the problems facing the city of Rome, too large by Italian standards and difficult to administer, whereas in the South the two regions of Campania and Calabria show the worst indicators, particularly the homicide rate (which will be discussed in the next section).

Recent work by Giorgio Nuzzo has shown that some convergence of regional social indicators has taken place over time, as shown in Table 6.2.[5] Firstly, the North-East of the country stands out as the area enjoying over the whole period the highest level of social capital, which

147

Table 6.1 Regional indicators of social capital, c. 2015

	Composite Index Social relations, Italy =100[a]	Electoral Participation 2014[b]	Voluntary activities, 2016[c]	Presence of non profit organizations 2011[d]	Length of civil trials 2014[e]	Homicides rate 2015[f]
Piemonte	101	67	12	59	200	0.5
Valle d'Aosta	109	50	15	104	113	0.8
Liguria	102	61	11	60	269	0.6
Lombardia	104	66	14	47	228	0.6
Trentino Alto Adige	122	53	24	100	158	0.5
Veneto	109	64	17	59	299	0.3
Friuli Venezia Giulia	108	58	14	82	185	0.7
Emilia-Romagna	103	70	11	58	252	0.5
Toscana	104	67	11	65	357	0.5
Umbria	101	70	11	71	435	0.9
Marche	99	66	12	69	327	0.3
Lazio	96	56	8	43	419	0.6
Abruzzo	94	64	8	55	367	0.5
Molise	89	55	9	58	525	0.3
Campania	78	51	6	25	610	1.8
Puglia	84	51	7	37	626	0.8
Basilicata	90	49	8	56	750	0.2
Calabria	79	46	7	41	757	1.9
Sicilia	84	43	6	40	561	1.0
Sardegna	96	43	10	59	444	1.1
Regions						
North	105	65	14	58	236	0.5
Centre	99	62	10	56	393	0.5
South	84	49	7	38	597	1.2
ITALY	**97**	**59**	**11**	**51**	**420**	**0.8**

Source: Istat, *Rapporto sul BES*, 2016

[a] Includes family and friends relations, social and political participation, voluntary activities, funding of non profit organizations

[b] per 100 adult population

[c] per 100 people > 14 years of age

[d] per 10,000 inhabitants

[e] average length in days

[f] per 100,000 inhabitants

is coherent with the established predominance in this area of SMEs, requiring for their existence functioning networks and widespread relationships of trust. Secondly, the mountainous regions Valle d'Aosta and Trentino-Alto Adige (but also Friuli and Umbria) are those regions with the highest level of social capital, chiefly for geographical reasons (the widespread existence of common lands). This confirms the picture already presented in Table 6.1. It can also be noted that the three core northwestern regions (Piemonte, Lombardia, Liguria) have lost ground while the two largest northeastern regions (Veneto and Emilia-Romagna) have gained ground over time. Among the central regions, Marche shows a marked improvement, connected with the increasing diffusion of industrial districts, while in Lazio difficulties remain entrenched, as mentioned above. In the South, the most spectacular improvements have taken place in Abruzzo and Sardinia, which correspond to their economic improvement, while the worst performance is that of Campania, as already noted in Table 6.1. Nuzzo's work defeats the idea that social capital is resistant to any change, although it remains true that the historical legacy matters.

The regional analysis of social capital offers additional evidence of the profound dualism between North and South that exists in Italy. This is a cultural and civil dualism above any economic one. The historical origin of such cultural dualism goes back to the Middle Ages with the Italian city-states' tradition of self-government in the North-centre (excluding Rome) on one side and the unification of the South under foreign autocratic rule supported by a local landed elite on the other. This produced a southern population alienated from a distant state, a lack of trust in public institutions that were "extractive" (to use Acemoglu's term), a readiness to accept (and pay for) protection offered by local leaders, and a lack of organized civil society, which autocratic rule prevented from flourishing. At unification, it was far from easy to put in place more favourable social (and educational, as we saw in the previous chapter) conditions, not least because it took a long time for northerners to realize how in-built and long-lasting this different culture was. The single most important factor

Table 6.2 Synthetic indicator of social capital in the regions, 1901–2001 (Italy = 100)

	1901	1951	2001
Piemonte	127	121	105
Valle d'Aosta	145	167	149
Lombardia	122	118	110
Trentino-Alto Adige	550	398	206
Veneto	99	105	125
Friuli Venezia Giulia	131	129	135
Liguria	119	104	105
Emilia-Romagna	115	121	127
Toscana	119	133	125
Umbria	107	111	137
Marche	67	112	124
Lazio	93	81	80
Abruzzo	49	64	107
Molise	72	74	89
Campania	44	54	43
Puglia	61	68	75
Basilicata	57	56	83
Calabria	39	54	65
Sicilia	63	67	82
Sardegna	38	80	109
Regions			
North-West	124	117	108
North-East	164	139	135
Centre	106	109	105
South	52	63	81
ITALY	**100**	**100**	**100**

Source: G. Nuzzo, 2006

running against change has been the strengthening position of organized crime, which remained under the surface during the fascist period as a result of the authoritarian government's extensive police controls, but which exploded after the Second World War. The Italian research on this topic is huge so pressures of space determine that I can only give an overview of the most important aspects of Italian organized crime.

MAFIA AND CORRUPTION

In an influential book published in 1958, the American political scientist Edward Banfield coined the term "amoral familism" to describe the self-interested, family-centric behaviour widespread in southern Italy (which was later to be defined as "bonding social capital", as mentioned above).[6] This family-centric society placed the well-being of the family group (including not only those connected by blood, but also through other bonds) above the public good and the rights of their fellow citizens, and were prepared to use corrupt and illegal means to further their group interests. Banfield suggested that this type of behaviour was due to the absence of community-building institutions, the lack of a state interested in building up and enforcing the rule of law (in the period prior to unification), and the predominance of self-interested landed elites. In the wake of Banfield's work, research on organized crime and its social, political and economic impact has grown immensely, and the Italian state's capability to control organized crime has improved, even if it remains incapable of eradicating the phenomenon.

Of course, organized crime does not exist only in Italy, but in many other countries around the world. Italy, however, has criminal organizations that are also active abroad. The most significant of these local organizations are the Camorra (active in Naples and Campania), the Cosa Nostra (in Sicily) and the 'Ndrangheta (in Calabria) (referred to as "CCN" in the following). The word "mafia" is generally used as a label for all criminal groups acting illegally in an organized way,[7] including CCN as well as others. In a country with low overall rates of homicide, the high homicide rates in Campania, Calabria and Sicily, shown in Table 6.1, is testimony to their use of violence.

Although Sicily is no longer the worst region for killings, there was a period in the 1980s and 1990s during which the Sicilian mafia tried to attack the state, murdering both judges and politicians who fought against them. Perhaps the most famous case is that of the judge Giovanni Falcone, who struck the first major blow against Cosa Nostra, setting up a "maxi-trial" against 706 members, which when completed in January 1992 resulted in 19 life-sentences and a total of 2,665 years of jail. Falcone was murdered by the Cosa Nostra a few months later, on 23 May, in a bombing that also killed his wife and his escort; 57 days later his friend and collaborator Paolo Borsellino was also killed. This marked the beginning of a strong reaction from the Italian state that was, in a few years, to bring an end to mafia attacks on the state. Killings today mostly take place inside mafias, arising from internal disputes and the dominance of one family over another, and are more widespread in Campania and Calabria than in Sicily. This unfortunately does not mean that Cosa Nostra has disappeared, but that they have learned how to act through other means, as we shall see below, in the areas where they are rooted and also by building up networks of corruption across the entire country.

The first important thing to note about the Italian mafia is that it is an historical phenomenon that, in parts of southern Italy, goes back long before the unification of the country and that arose out of conditions that had been developed over centuries.[8] There are different views about the exact origin of CCN, but historians agree that criminal behaviour on behalf of the family and against other families and the state can already be found in these areas in the twelfth and thirteenth centuries. However, recent work by the Italian scholar, Francesco Benigno, has argued that use of present-day names is not so old and can be disputed in terms of their etymological origin.[9] The first to be mentioned in the criminal records is Camorra, to designate criminal rackets in Naples in the first half of the nineteenth century. Indeed, the term was known abroad as illustrated in a letter from the British Prime Minister William Gladstone to his colleague

Lord Aberdeen, when visiting the Bourbon kingdom, which described the terrible state of the prisons in Naples where some "Camorristi" (members of the Camorra) were housed. The word "mafia" started to appear in connection with Sicilian criminality a bit later in the 1860s, while the word 'Ndrangheta has been in use since the 1880s.

The kind of criminal activity in which they specialize varies over time and among organizations. The most recent report estimates, in 2011, the total revenues from illicit markets in the EU at €110 billion, or 0.9 per cent of EU GDP. Surprisingly, Italy, at 1 per cent nationally, is only just slightly above the EU average, surpassed by Latvia (2.8%), Romania and Cyprus (1.9%), Lithuania, Bulgaria and Greece (1.6%), Malta (1.4%), Slovakia (1.3%), Estonia (1.2%), but also by Austria, Hungary, Ireland, Slovenia (1.1%) and is on a par with Spain. The UK is at 0.9 per cent, France at 0.8 per cent and Germany at 0.7 per cent.[10] In Italy it is both true that other criminal organizations often led by non-Italians are active in the country and share Italian illicit markets,[11] and that CCN also collect revenues from abroad. Table 6.3 details the sources of illicit revenues: drugs, extortion and racketeering (in Italy called "*pizzo*"), counterfeiting and usury are the four largest sources of revenue, followed by prostitution and fraud (at the expense of Italian authorities, but also of the EU). The 'Ngrangheta is today recognized as one of the leaders of cocaine trafficking in Europe, while Italian mafias are only indirectly involved in street-based prostitution, which is mostly controlled by Eastern European and African gangs. The Camorra is active in illegal gambling, counterfeiting and the illegal trade in tobacco products. The major source of revenues for Italian mafias in Italy is recognized to be extortion, racketeering and fraud.

All criminal activities have a negative economic and social impact, but the *pizzo* is terribly invasive. The payment of protection money by legitimate businesses threatened by mafia members keeps entire territories under mafia control. Refusal to pay has resulted in killings and today those (not very many) who have had the courage to denounce mafia members to the police have to be protected by bodyguards. Efforts by the police to discover these rackets are concerted and inquisitorial. Many mafiosi have been jailed and their assets confiscated and granted to NGOs[12] and social cooperatives to be administered in the interest of the community, but the diffusion of these criminal organizations in Calabria, Campania and Sicilia is too pervasive to be eradicated unless the local civil society increases its willingness to revolt.[13]

Table 6.3 Estimated yearly revenue from illicit markets, c. 2011

	Million $	share
Drugs	5,348	18.1
Trafficking of human beings	3,082	10.5
Illicit trafficking in firearms	93	0.3
Illicit trade in tobacco products	546	1.9
Counterfeiting	4,596	15.6
Illegal gambling	425	1.4
Extortion/racketeering	5,253	17.8
Usury	4,634	15.7
Fraud	2,959	10.0
Other	2,544	8.7
TOTAL	**29,480**	**100.0**

Source: Savona & Riccardi 2015

Fraud is another particularly invasive crime, often involving professional people and public authorities, entangled with corruption activities and spreading far beyond the traditional areas of mafia businesses through money laundering. Coffee shops, restaurants, construction companies, retail trade, transport, logistics, hotels, real estate companies across Italy are acquired and managed by members of the mafia or its friends, using mafia money, creating a whole sector in which the mafias exercise legal activities supported through its illegal activities. The high level of corruption to be found in Italy, especially in the mafia regions (see Table 3.18 in Chapter 3), is due to their existence, which requires the complicity of public officers in order for them to be able to carry out extortions and frauds. This support for corruption by criminal organizations diminishes the willingness of citizens to act against illegality.[14]

Wherever there is a flow of public money, be it through tenders to build infrastructure or health expenditure or social transfers, the mafia is ready to organize corruption and fraud. Illicit waste management by the Camorra, famously exposed by the Italian writer, Roberto Saviano, is one of the most dangerous frauds, polluting entire areas and producing great damage to the health of local populations.[15] Ever since the publication of Saviano's book he has lived under police protection. In recent years, even the migrant crisis has been an opportunity for mafia exploitation, with mafia organizations setting up reception facilities in an attempt to divert public funds. Fortunately, the deliberately fragmented network of reception facilities has limited the opportunities for criminality, but it serves to illustrate the capability of the mafia to exploit all possible opportunities for fraud.[16]

As I have said, research measuring the negative impact of criminal organizations and corruption is extensive.[17] If we add that in the areas where this culture is widespread unemployment and poverty are also endemic, we can better understand how difficult it is to resist organized crime, determining a vicious circle: more organized crime leads to less investment and greater unemployment; more unemployment leads to less capability to resist organized crime. But it is also important to mention that some southern Italians are both victims and executioners, as happens in all vicious circles. Victims, because so many are oppressed by the mafia, but also executioners, because local elites are complicit and not doing enough to change the status quo, as Emanuele Felice has argued in his book *Why the South has Remained Behind*.[18] No doubt, central government and the rest of the country have not helped enough in supporting southern civil society to rid themselves of this historical legacy, but the first to seek to change the situation should have been the southern elites themselves. I believe that today's highly mobile population will help reduce the flow of many young people to the mafia gangs, but support for the local civil society opposing the mafia remains a priority.

THE STRENGTH OF CIVIL SOCIETY

As we saw in Chapter 4, the third sector in Italy is quite significant. In this section I will briefly illustrate its composition, with the help of Table 6.4, which shows that in the 2011 census NPOs (non-profit organizations) numbered around 300,000[19] with almost 1 million paid employees, revenues of €64 billion and 4.7 million full-time equivalent voluntary workers.[20] Of these NPOs, two-thirds are devoted to cultural, sports and leisure activities, including some environmental activities.[21] Italy has countless organizations, many of them very powerful,[22] that offer various services related to Italy's immense cultural heritage (accounting for around 60 per cent of all voluntary activity). In terms of revenue and paid employees, education and research, health and social assistance command the lion's share as these NPOs have a more entrepreneurial approach, really being "social enterprises" (associations, foundations and social cooperatives).[23] It has been calculated that these enterprises (some 20,000, 7% of the total) make up 45 per cent of total revenues. In 1997 they benefited from legislation that granted substantial tax allowances specifically related to their social relevance[24] and since then they have experienced rapid growth, able to collect public and private income, often through fund-raising activities, in addition to the direct revenues stemming from the sale of their services. In 2006, further legislation was passed in favour of NPOs, the so-called "5 × 1000", which allowed Italian citizens, in their annual income tax declaration, to instruct the central revenues agency to pay 5 × 1000 (or 0.5%) of their tax payment to a NPO of their choice.[25]

It is important to note that the 1991 law on social cooperatives[26] defines two types: type A, which delivers social services, and type B, which gives work to disadvantaged people, be they physically or mentally handicapped, or socially marginalized (drug-users, people coming out of prison,

Table 6.4 The Italian third sector, 2011

	No. of units %	Paid employees %	Voluntary workers %	Revenues %
Culture, sport, leisure	65	19	59	16
Education, research	5	17	4	13
Health	4	19	7	18
Social assistance	8	28	13	16
Environment	2	1	3	1
Human rights, politics, trade unionism	8	6	6	10
Economic development	4	9	3	9
Religion	2	...	3	2
Foundations, philanthropy	2	1	2	15
TOTALS	301,191	951,580	4,758,622[a]	63,940 (million euros)

Source: Istat 2011 census of non profit organizations

Notes: [a] full time equivalent voluntary personnel declared by the NP organizations

youngsters and women who have suffered abuse and the like). These type B social cooperatives often work with for-profit firms to provide labour intensive kinds of subsidized employment, and in addition have helped to build communities where productive activities are developed. One of the reasons why the migrant emergency has not caused major dislocation to the country has been the availability of social cooperatives, some of which have specialized in the care of migrants.

Since 1972 Italy has also benefited from the widespread presence of the Catholic organization Caritas (also active in other countries). Every diocese in Italy (220) has a Caritas, which organizes charitable services for the poor, including catering, accommodation, microcredit facilities, delivery of foodstuffs, childcare and help for old people and migrants, as well as projects aimed at providing jobs and support for families in difficulty, refuges for abused women, and legal and medical assistance. The central offices of Caritas produce each year several reports: one on poverty, another one monitoring the effectiveness of public policies against poverty, and a highly regarded report on immigration through the Migrantes foundation. All Italian Catholic parishes are mobilized in support of the local Caritas, either directly through voluntary activity or indirectly by providing funds.

In recent years there has been a substantial increase in social activities by third-sector organizations, which goes a long way towards explaining why the country has not been disarticulated by the worst economic crisis in its existence.[27] Also, it must be noted that the "social economy" (the third sector, cooperatives and mutuals combined) have the propensity to cultivate at the local level traditions and communities, producing "social cohesion" and defeating the alienation widespread where the social economy is weak. Social capital is nurtured by the social economy and its effects spill over on to the rest of the capitalist economy, attracting investment, promoting employment and innovation.[28]

Conclusion

If there is a place overflowing with history it is Italy. I do not mean simply a country with a long past – there are many other nations that share that distinction. Rather, history in Italy permeates and shapes the present and is living still in its cities, in its churches, palaces, banks; in its squares that host markets, religious celebrations, political gatherings, social and leisure activities; in its care for the landscape, both natural and artistic. A monastery vacated by friars can be turned into a hospital, then into a prison, then into a university building (as in Bologna), with a tireless effort to reinterpret monuments rather than discard them.

The relationship between economic activity and communities at a local and regional level is perhaps one of Italy's most distinct and established characteristics. It has found many interpreters, such as the celebrated entrepreneur Adriano Olivetti[1] and the economist Giacomo Becattini.[2] Olivetti was as much a "civil" entrepreneur, a thinker and a promoter of culture, as he was a businessman. In his 1945 book, *L'ordine politico delle Comunità* (*The Political Order of Communities*) he argued that the entrepreneur's role was to trigger the wider economic, social and cultural development of the region and community where its factory was located. He established the movement Community to promote these ideas and was even elected to parliament as a representative of that movement. Although his early death at the age of 59 did not allow him to consolidate either his company or his movement, the "humanistic" management that he exemplified is still alive today and has inspired many other entrepreneurs, who want to keep faith with this *genius loci*. Indeed, his legacy was recognized by Unesco in 2018, with Ivrea (Piedmont) – Olivetti's city – becoming Italy's latest world heritage site.

Becattini was the most coherent theorist of territory as the unit of inspiration for economic activity with a unique and non-replicable identity. His view of the market economy was as follows:

If each place produces the goods that can only be produced in that place – as a result of its landscape, its culture, its arts, its identity – in so doing guaranteeing the self-reproduction of the community living in such place, then the exchange of goods among the world's local systems will not cause domination, hierarchy and exploitation, but through cooperative competition and respecting identities and differences, will produce mutual development, high quality of life and public happiness.[3]

The strength of SMEs and social enterprises in Italy, which we discussed in Chapters 4–6, stem from this root: the centuries old habit of becoming highly specialized in one type of production through division of labour and exchange, coupled with a responsibility towards the local region to make investments to facilitate community well-being. As long as the world was organized in local systems, Italy could flourish. It was relatively easy for Italian entrepreneurs to produce goods to be exported, but when globalization triumphed after the 1980s and big business became no longer the American exception but the rule, the Italian economy started to suffer. As I have shown, Italy's response to globalization has been inadequate.

It first refused to face the challenge, trying instead to lean on the "small is beautiful" ethos; at the same time, it mismanaged its public finances and accumulated a huge public debt in the 1980s. When reforms proved inevitable, it muddled through by liquidating state enterprises before finally finding out how best to face the challenges of globalization. As a result

Italy's few areas of big business are surviving with difficulty, some remain under state control while others have fallen under foreign control. Then the financial crisis came and Italy lost 25 per cent of its manufacturing output, dragging down GDP, which by 2016 had not recovered to its 2008 level. It is true that Italian governments have blamed austerity measures imposed by the EU for this fall, and there is some truth in these complaints over the short term, but the real longer-term issue, which the financial crisis has compelled Italy to come to terms with, is that Italy's small firms cannot internationalize and much less attract highly educated people. Fortunately, Italians are highly adaptable people, having survived under many different political and economic regimes, and are now showing a great willingness to try new paths, which can be seen in the propensity to build new political parties, to organize civil society enterprises, and to carry out reforms.

To find a new equilibrium will not be a short-term undertaking, but Italy has a winning card:[4] its medium-sized companies. They combine the territorial root outlined above with a drive to internationalize. They are highly specialized in the production of specific goods, sold all over the world, and are capable of buying other mid-size companies in their field in other countries, forming the pocket multinationals we described in Chapter 4. I do not believe that Italy is currently in a position to bridge its gap in big business and for this reason Italy is committed to seeing the EU flourish and in building relationships with French and German big business. But if the Italian medium-sized companies continue to grow, things will certainly change in the future. The present priority for Italy is therefore to strengthen its mid-size companies and consolidate its few remaining big ones. Also, a more creative and international interpretation of its position in the Mediterranean would help the development of the South. But all this requires the reintroduction of strategic thinking on the part of government, something that does not appear likely at present, and not only in Italy.

Meanwhile, the country can become the champion of the "civil economy" economic model, which retains the local identity of its regions, which continues to invest in community facilities, which believes in keeping alive traditions and family-social relations, and which works towards social cohesion and above all inclusiveness. Civil economy draws on a tradition of economic and philosophical thought that has its roots in the Aristotelian thinking reworked by Franciscan and Dominican schools in the Middle Ages, and then by the Humanists, up to the Milanese and Neapolitan Enlightenment Schools of Beccaria, Verri, Genovesi and Dragonetti.[5] Unlike the Anglo-Saxon political economy tradition, civil economy rejects the separation of the market – the place of self-interest – from social relations – the place of friendship. The civil economy view of the market is positive if it is based on reciprocity, on "mutual aid" and not on self-interest alone. Only if self-interest is embedded inside the more comprehensive common interest of all participants can the market be the source of "good life".

Today's global network of multinationals interested only in profit maximization and which locate and relocate their factories with little regard for local communities, culture and traditions, is increasingly questioned by public opinion. This global capitalism is proficient at meeting basic material needs, but coupled with its financial arm and its digital platforms it breeds increasing inequalities, destroying societies and crowding out authentic democracy. It also jeopardizes interpersonal relations and diminishes public happiness. If Italy succeeds in keeping its territorially and community based model of business alive and competitive, it will offer, together with other European countries also engaged in the preservation and promotion of their native cultural environments, an alternative way to the wild globalization that currently predominates – a way that brings economics back to its role as an instrument catering for public happiness and not for the concentration of wealth in the hands of a few.

Notes

1. INTRODUCING THE ITALIAN ECONOMY

1. For an extensive treatment of the evolution of the Italian economy from unification to the 1980s, see Zamagni, *The Economic History of Italy 1860–1990*.
2. See Ciocca, "Brigantaggio ed economia nel Mezzogiorno d'Italia, 1860–1870".
3. On the long-run evolution of the Italian South, see Perrotta & Sunna, *L'arretratezza del Mezzogiorno. Le idee, l'economia, la storia*. On the comparative situation at unification, see Zamagni, "La situazione economico-sociale del Mezzogiorno negli anni dell'unificazione".

2. THE ITALIAN ECONOMIC STORY, 1946–2016

1. Some killings could not be prevented, but there was no generalized revenge against those who had been part of the fascist party which ruled the northern part of the country under German occupation. Prosecutions of people guilty of major crimes were few.
2. See Zamagni, *Economic History of Italy 1860–1990*.
3. There is now a full account of the history of IRI and its achievements in six volumes, *Storia dell'IRI* published by Laterza (2012–16).
4. Zamagni, *Finmeccanica. Competenze che vengono da lontano*. As much as one third of Italian engineering companies had ended up in this IRI sub-holding.
5. See Zamagni, *An Economic History of Europe Since 1700*. The secret negotiations among representatives of the European Christian Democratic parties (then in power) that took place in Switzerland in 1946–9 and which debated, among other things, the formation of ECSC and a customs union, saw the active participation of Italian DC members.

6. Fiocco, *L'Italia prima del miracolo economico. L'inchiesta parlamentare sulla miseria 1951–54.*

7. Bagnasco, *Tre Italie: la problematica territoriale dello sviluppo italiano.*

8. On this theme, see Antonelli *et al.*, *Innovazione tecnologica e sviluppo industriale nel secondo dopoguerra.*

9. See Pugliese, *L'Italia tra migrazioni internazionali e migrazioni interne.*

10. See Lepre, *Storia della prima repubblica. L'Italia dal 1942 al 1992.*

11. For the Red Brigades and other, less important, revolutionary groups there is a large literature. In English, see Alexander & Pluchinsky, *Europe's Red Terrorists: The Fighting Communist Organizations.*

12. The PCI and the leftist trade union CGIL were slow in condemning the extremism of the Red Brigades, a mistake they were to later recognize.

13. This sliding scale was abolished in 1984.

14. The instigator of the killing of Giorgio Ambrosoli, Michele Sindona, was later jailed. He committed suicide in prison in 1986.

15. The PCI became a reformist party in 1991, with the name of Partito Democratico della Sinistra (PDS).

16. The details of this sad story can be found in Zamagni, *L'industria chimica italiana e l'IMI.*

17. We should remember that until the reforms of 2003 Germany was considered "the sick man of Europe" and that Italian per capita income in 2003 was only five percentage points below the German one, while the British figure had shot up as a result of the flourishing finance markets at the time. The French rate was at the same level as the Italian one.

18. Romano Prodi was a professor of economics at the University of Bologna, who had served as president of IRI (1982–89). In 1995 he launched the Ulivo (Olive Tree), a coalition between the PDS and the smaller parties heir to the DC. The Ulivo won the 1996 elections and he became prime minister (1996–98). He became president of the EU Commission (1999–2004) and then prime minister for a second time (2006–08). On the Italian politics of these years, see Di Nucci, *La democrazia distributiva. Saggio sul sistema politico dell'Italia repubblicana.*

19. The election was won by Partito Democratico (PD), which arose from a merger of the parties of the Ulivo coalition.

20. In 2003 Germany also reformed the labour market alongside a reform of welfare that produced much better results than the Italian one. The real divergence in performance of the two economies started then.

21. "Fourth" because it developed after the "first", capitalism tout-court, the "second", state capitalism, and the "third", of the industrial districts.

3. MEASURING THE ITALIAN ECONOMY

1. Baffigi, *Il PIL per la storia d'Italia. Istruzioni per l'uso*. I have been part of the research team of the Bank of Italy project, with responsibility for the reconstruction of value added data in services.

2. An overview of the demographic changes in Italy can be found in Salvini & De Rose, *Rapporto sulla popolazione. L'Italia a 150 anni dall'Unità*.

3. Japan ranked much lower. It is well-known that Japanese productivity per hour worked is low and is offset by longer hours of work.

4. This process is studied in Felice, *Perchè il Sud è rimasto indietro*.

5. Macchiati, *Perchè l'Italia cresce poco*.

6. Istat estimates it at 12 per cent, because it does not include the "criminal" economy.

7. Italy is actually in a period of transition between the two systems.

8. In the South the organization of hospitals can be less than acceptable, but citizens are able to receive treatment in the North. For more on the Italian health service, see Toth, *La sanità in Italia*.

9. Luigi Einaudi (1874–1961) was a famous economist active before the First World War and then marginalized by fascism. After the demise of fascism, he was appointed governor of the Bank of Italy, then minister of the treasury and then president of the republic.

10. Public debt did not grow because of increasing inflation, see Tables 3.6 and 3.11.

11. See Kaufmann, Kraay & Mastruzzi, "The WGI: Methodology and Analytical Issues".

12. See Charron, Dijkstra & Lapuente, "Mapping the Regional Divide in Europe: A Measure for Assessing Quality of Government in 2016 European Regions".

13. The graph shows that Turkey has a similar spread.

14. For an application of this approach to Italian provinces, see Nifo & Vecchione, "Do Institutions Play a Role in Skilled Migration? The Case of Italy". In this work, the authors argue that the regions with the worst EQI lose young people to the universities of the regions with higher EQI.

15. See, for example, Diaz del Hoyo *et al.*, "Real Convergence in the Euro Area" and also Masuch, Moshammer & Pierluigi, "Institutions, Public Debt and Growth in Europe". Variable "public debt" is also included in these econometric exercises. This article concludes: "The findings of the paper support the view that the quality of institutions is an important determinant of average per capita GDP growth during the last 23 years. The results seem particularly important for countries where institutional delivery is below or around the EU average and initial public debt is above a threshold (e.g. 60 or 70%)" (20).

4. THE FORM OF THE ITALIAN ECONOMY

1. The entire economy (excluding public administration and non-profit enterprises) had, in 2011, an average firm size equal to 3.7 employees.

2. The best work on the period to 1971 is Giannetti & Vasta, *Evolution of the Italian Enterprises in the Twentieth Century*.

3. Fuà & Zacchia, *Industrializzazione senza fratture*.

4. Becattini has been the most prolific author, with a number of publications in English. See Becattini, "The Marshallian Industrial Districts as a Socio-Economic Notion" and Becattini, Bellandi & De Propris, *A Handbook of Industrial Districts*.

5. Brusco, *Piccole imprese e distretti industriali*.

6. The Italian literature on industrial districts is huge. Among the best books are Fortis & Quadrio Curzio, *Industria e distretti. Un paradigma di perdurante competitività italiana* and Omiccioli, *I sistemi produttivi locali. Trasformazioni fra globalizzazione e crisi*, which examines the manufacturing style of cities and the connection between industrial districts and global value chains.

7. Not at the level of single companies, because the companies included (as well as the municipalities) are not constant.

8. This trend was apparent before the crisis and had given rise to an expectation of decline of the industrial districts. For this approach, see Onida, *Se il piccolo non cresce. Piccole e medie imprese italiane in affanno*.

9. For the reasons mentioned, the number of industrial districts monitored by different organizations does not coincide with the Istat's numbers.

10. See also Lombardi & Magliocchi, "Distretti industriali tra mutamento territoriale, economico e profili d'impresa".

11. The Mediobanca research centre has later cooperated with the research centre of Unioncamere, the central office of the Italian chambers of commerce, chiefly because the collection of budget data as the basis of all the statistical elaborations is done by Unioncamere. The Mediobanca research centre has been led for many years by Fulvio Coltorti, who has produced countless presentations of the results, which are available on the Mediobanca website: www.mbres.it. An English publication from this source is Coltorti *et al.*, *Midsized Manufacturing Companies: The New Driver of Italian Competitiveness*.

12. The main reasons for these changes are that these enterprises grow and pass over to the set of medium-large enterprises, or they are sold to foreign investors. The instances of shrinking and of failures are much less evident.

13. Excluding imports of energy products.

14. Excluding imports of energy products.

15. The Netherlands is not considered, because its huge surplus is mostly made

up of transit trade, the result of its port hubs for shipping commodities out of Europe.

16. Fortis, *The Pillars of the Italian Economy: Manufacturing, Food and Wine, Tourism*. See also Giunta & Rossi, *Che cosa sa fare l'Italia. La nostra economia dopo la grande crisi*.

17. For a long-run view of fashion in Italy, see Muzzarelli, *Breve storia della moda in Italia*.

18. Today the Benetton family is no longer only in the clothing sector, but in many others, including highways. See Favero, *Benetton. I colori del successo*.

19. For example, Italy has a buttons district in the Bergamo province with 150 enterprises.

20. Italian agriculture was never capable of producing enough for domestic consumption, because of the limited presence of plains in the country. Today processed food and wine of high quality are winning export markets. For a summary presentation of Italian agriculture, see Fanfani, *Il sistema agroalimentare in Italia: i grandi cambiamenti e le tendenze recenti*.

21. In 1981 an association was created in France called "Les Henokiens" (from Henoch, the great biblical patriarch), in which companies over 200 years old, still in existence and under the management or control of the family of the founder, could enrol. Out of the 46 members, Italy has 12.

22. See Zamagni, "L'industria chimica". Totalling the turnover of the top 20 Italian chemical SMEs, we reach €17 billion in 2013. Each of them is cultivating a highly specialized niche, with an innovative approach in terms of developing new products for their clients and a special attention to the use of raw materials alternative to oil derivatives.

23. For a summary, see Colli, *The History of Family Business 1850–2000* and Colli & Perez, *The Endurance of Large Family Businesses Around the World*.

24. These and other considerations on the problems of SMEs can be found in Onida, *Se il piccolo non cresce. Piccole e medie imprese italiane in affanno*.

25. I have written elsewhere about Unipol: see my biography of Enea Mazzoli, president of Unipol for a crucial period of its growth, *Come si è affermata la grande impresa cooperativa in Italia. Il contributo di Enea Mazzoli*.

26. On the Fiat-Chrysler affair, see Berta, *Fiat Chrysler e la deriva dell'Italia industriale*.

27. The present chairman of Exor John Elkann, is no exception. His surname is not Agnelli, because his mother is an Agnelli married to an Elkann.

28. Not much exists in English. See Clark, *Mondo Agnelli: Fiat, Chrysler and the Power of a Dynasty* and Garuzzo, *Fiat: The Secrets of an Epoch*. Garuzzo was a high-level manager of Fiat.

29. However, 30 per cent of its capital is owned by CDP and 35.5 per cent has been sold to the market.

30. See the six volume series *Storia dell'IRI*. The volumes giving a more comprehensive view are: Russolillo, *Un gruppo singolare. Settori, bilanci, presenza nell'economia italiana* and Ciocca, *L'IRI nell'economia italiana*.

31. Fincantieri is still under state control through Fintecna, owned by CDP, formally a joint-stock company, but 80 per cent controlled by the Italian ministry of economy and finance, which has become the strategic fund of the Italian state.

32. Thirty per cent of Leonardo is controlled by the Italian ministry of economy and finance. Finmeccanica also administered Alfa-Romeo, which was sold to Fiat in 1988. On Finmeccanica, see Zamagni, *Finmeccanica. Competenze che vengono da lontano*.

33. See Giacalone, *Razza corsara. Mercati mal controllati e la politica in fuga. Il caso Telecom e la mala privatizzazione*.

34. The worst case is the Taranto steel mill which had to be repurchased by the state and resold to a more capable enterprise.

35. See Clô, *ENI 1953-2003*.

36. This shortage of coal and oil in Italy has induced the country to save on energy intensive processes of production. See on this Malanima, *Energy Consumption in Italy in the 19th and 20th Centuries* and also Toninelli, "Energy and the Puzzle of Italy's Economic Growth".

37. This referendum produced a great loss for Finmeccanica as well, because it had reunified under its control the entire production capacity of nuclear plants.

38. See Mise (Ministry of Economic Development), 2017. Hydroelectricity accounts for 40 per cent of the renewable sources. Adding non-electrical uses of energy sources, renewables cover 18 per cent of the total.

39. This is of course paradoxical: having banned nuclear plants, Italy now imports electricity from countries that use nuclear plants.

40. The account of this Italian history of excellence is now available, mostly written by the same engineers who have founded or managed such companies: Cariati *et al.*, *Storia delle società italiane di ingegneria e impiantistica*.

41. See Barucci & Pierobon, *Le privatizzazioni in Italia*.

42. I have written the long history of Italcementi, a company whose origin goes back to 1863, up to the internationalization drive of the early 1990s; see Zamagni, *Italcementi. Dalla leadership nazionale all'internazionalizzazione*.

43. To my knowledge, this is the only case in the world.

44. See Zamagni, *Come si è affermata la grande impresa cooperativa in Italia. Il contributo di Enea Mazzoli*. The role of cooperatives in Italy is actually larger, because of the indirect employment they generate.

45. Companies legally recorded as cooperatives are many more, because in Italy

it is not compulsory for a cooperative to belong to an umbrella organization. But all the cooperatives outside ACI are little known, smallish and more often than not fake cooperatives. This is a situation which ACI is fighting against.

46. In 2017, of the 20 largest companies in Bologna, 11 were cooperatives.

47. In 1988 the market share of saving banks was 23 per cent, of popular banks and credit unions 20 per cent; state banks stood at 18 per cent, the remaining share, 39 per cent was comprised of joint-stock companies, many of which were under IRI control.

48. The history of IMI has been published in five volumes by Il Mulino (1998–2010) under my editorial supervision.

49. The literal translation is "special" credit institutes (long-term), opposed to the "ordinary" credit banks (short-term)

50. Piluso, *Mediobanca tra regole e mercato*.

51. IMI got into trouble owing to the extended credit granted to some chemical firms.

52. On this see Mattesini & Messori, *L'evoluzione del Sistema bancario meridionale*.

53. The only real exception was the Monte dei Paschi (MPS) of Siena, the third largest of the Italian banks of the time and one of the oldest banks in the world (created in 1472) still in operation, found itself in trouble as a result of poor management.

54. At the time of writing (2017) the net amount of NPLs is €80 billion, covered by a collateral worth €122 billion which cannot be rapidly recovered.

55. Even deposits above €100,000 could be lost in principle, if this was necessary to cover banks losses. This mechanism went into operation while Italy had to face the insolvency of some of its popular banks (Veneto Banca, Banca Popolare di Vicenza, Banca Popolare dell'Etruria) and other banks (MPS; Cassa di Risparmio di Ferrara).

56. Today there is also a lot of Chinese-made souvenirs, but the difference is quite apparent.

57. It appears that in 2017 Italy has overtaken France, as a result of an unexpected boom of tourists.

58. Data from Eurostat, 2010.

59. According to a recent estimate, the "culture industry" in Italy, excluding education, accounts for 6 per cent of GDP directly. There is some overlapping with the estimate of VA in tourism, which has not been evaluated.

60. See Traclò & Tortorella, *Oltre i limiti del turismo all'italiana*.

61. Prometeia, *L'economia della bellezza. Quanto vale e qual è il suo potenziale*.

5. HUMAN FACTORS

1. A term coined by the anthropologist, Edward Banfield; see Chapter 6.

2. See Pugliese, *La terza età. Anziani e società in Italia.*

3. See Zamagni & Zamagni, *Famiglia e lavoro. Opposizione o armonia?*

4. See Livi Bacci, *Demografia del capitale umano.*

5. The creativity of Italian companies in this field is notable: they offer health check-ups, kindergartens or babysitting, care for the elderly, sports facilities, helpers to go shopping or buying medicines and the like, vacation facilities.

6. On the Italian tradition of company's welfare (mentioned in Chapter 4 in connection with Crespi d'Adda), see Mellinato & Varini, "Il welfare aziendale in Italia. Dalla storiografia a un caso di studio".

7. On this issue which is not only Italian (though it is quite pronounced in Italy) see Newman, *The Accordian Family: Boomerang Kids, Anxious Parents, and the Private Toll of Global Competition.*

8. On this topic, see Brandolini & Smeeding, "Inequality Patterns in Western Democracies: Cross-Country Differences and Changes Over Time".

9. See Zamagni, "L'offerta di istruzione in Italia 1861–1981". Illiteracy in the South in 1861 was at 90 per cent of the population over six years of age.

10. For other details on the construction of the index, see Felice & Vasta, "Passive Modernization? The New Human Development Index and its Components in Italy's Regions (1871–2007)".

11. On the unsatisfactory performance of indicators alternative to per capita GDP, see Felice, "The Misty Grail: the Search for a Comprehensive Measure of Development and the Reasons for GDP Primacy".

12. The public universities number 68. The only two important non-public universities are the Catholic University (with various campuses, the largest in Milan) and the Bocconi University, an economics and management university in Milan. There are 16 other smaller private institutions, plus 11 online universities.

13. Giannola, "Crisi del Mezzogiorno e nuove spinte migratorie".

14. This official figure, however, does not accurately reflect the total presence of foreign-born population in Italy, because it does not include the 410,000 foreigners who are legally in Italy, but not yet registered as residents, 200,000 asylum seekers, plus an estimated 400,000 illegal migrants.

15. The city of Prato, for instance, a famous textile city near Florence, is now full of Chinese firms which have taken over small businesses from the local population.

16. The aim is to build a European border with European coastal guards, using the most advanced electronic and satellite instruments.

6. SOCIAL FACTORS

1. See Bruni & Zamagni, *Civil Economy*.
2. Bourdieu, *Outline of a Theory of Practice*, Putnam, *Making Democracy Work* and De Blasio & Sestito, *Il capitale sociale. Che cos'è e cosa spiega*.
3. The literature also uses the concept of *civil capital*, which is identified with the institutions prevailing in a place. But again, institutions can be good or bad, as we saw in Chapter 3, and the ambiguity is not overcome.
4. Guiso, Sapienza & Zingales, "Civic Capital as the Missing Link".
5. Nuzzo, "Un secolo di statistiche sociali: persistenza o convergenza delle regioni italiane?". The author uses indicators of social and political participation, plus indicators of the level of trust. See also De Blasi & Nuzzo, "Historical Traditions of Civicness and Local Economic Development".
6. Banfield, *The Moral Basis of a Backward Society*.
7. Dickie, *Blood Brotherhoods: A History of Italy's Three Mafias*.
8. Among the first scholars to note this was Putnam, *Making Democracy Work*. He argued for a change in mentality and the building up of social capital in the southern regions.
9. Benigno, "La questione delle origini: mafia, camorra e storia d'Italia".
10. Savona & Riccardi, *From Illegal Markets to Legitimate Businesses. The Portfolio of Organized Crime in Europe*, 36.
11. The report mentions the presence of Chinese, Eastern European, Balkan and North African organizations active in Italy.
12. The most famous of these NGOs is Libera Terra, founded by the priest don Luigi Ciotti after the killings of Falcone and Borsellino.
13. Gambetta, *The Sicilian Mafia*.
14. See Fiorino & Galli, *La corruzione in Italia*.
15. Saviano, *Gomorrah* (a movie was also produced from the book).
16. One such example has been discovered in Rome and underwent trial with the title of "Mafia capitale". See issue no. 87 of *Meridiana* (2016) devoted to an analysis of this case.
17. See La Spina, *Mafia, legalità debole e sviluppo del Mezzogiorno*.
18. Felice, *Perchè il Sud è rimasto indietro*.
19. In reality, there are more NPOs, but some were inactive and others did not answer the census forms.
20. A thorough analysis of Italian voluntary activity can be found in Guidi, Fonović & Cappadozzi, *Volontari e attività volontarie*.
21. The category of environment by itself is small for this reason.
22. Italia Nostra, Fai, Cai, Legambiente, to name only a few.

23. For a general discussion of the results of the 2011 census of NPOs, see Barbetta, Ecchia & Zamaro, *Le istituzioni non-profit in Italia. Dieci anni dopo.*

24. The law defined an acronym for them, "Onlus" – Organizzazioni non governative di utilità sociale (non-profit organizations for social benefit).

25. I might mention that the same approach is used in Italy to support the Catholic church, with the 8 × 1000 tax contribution.

26. This was a path-breaking law. Many other European countries passed similar legislation later.

27. See Venturi & Rago, *Ri-Generare le Istituzioni. Il contributo dell'Economia Civile all'Innovazione istituzionale.*

28. See Sanna & De Bernardo, *Sviluppo locale e cooperazione sociale.*

CONCLUSION

1. Son of Camillo Olivetti, who had founded the typewriter firm Olivetti at the beginning of the twentieth century, Adriano (1901–60) not only made it a major company, but introduced a "humanistic" management, based on the promotion of the territories in which his plants were working.

2. Giacomo Becattini (1927–2017) was professor of economics at the University of Florence, where he created a school of territorial economics inspired by Alfred Marshall together with the Italian enlightenment schools and with particular application to Tuscan industry.

3. Becattini, *La coscienza di luogo nel recente pensiero di Giacomo Becattini*, 22 (my translation).

4. Magnani, *Terra e buoi dei paesi tuoi. Scuola, ricerca, ambiente, cultura, capitale umano: quando l'impresa investe nel territorio* speaks of the "secret arm" of the Italian economy, secret because it is not well covered by the press abroad. In his book he delivers innumerable examples of highly competitive territorially based medium-sized firms.

5. Bruni & Zamagni, *Civil Economy.*

References

Alexander, Y. & D. Pluchinsky, *Europe's Red Terrorists: The Fighting Communist Organizations*. London: Routledge, 1992.

Antonelli, C. et al., *Innovazione tecnologica e sviluppo industriale nel secondo dopoguerra*. Roma-Bari: Laterza, 2007.

Baffigi, A., *Il PIL per la storia d'Italia. Istruzioni per l'uso*. Venice: Marsilio, 2015.

Bagnasco, A., *Tre Italie: la problematica territoriale dello sviluppo italiano*. Bologna: Il Mulino, 1977.

Banfield, E., *The Moral Basis of a Backward Society*. Northampton, MA: Free Press, 1958.

Barbetta, G., G. Ecchia & N. Zamaro (eds), *Le istituzioni non-profit in Italia. Dieci anni dopo*. Bologna: Il Mulino, 2016.

Barucci, E. & F. Pierobon, *Le privatizzazioni in Italia*. Rome: Carocci, 2007.

Battilani, P., *Vacanze di pochi, vacanze di tutti*. Bologna: Il Mulino, 2009.

Becattini, G., "The Marshallian Industrial Districts as a Socio-Economic Notion", in F. Pyke, G. Becattini & W. Sengenberger (eds), *Industrial Districts and Interfirm Co-operation in Italy*, 37–51.Geneva: ILO, 1990.

Becattini, G., *La coscienza dei luoghi. Il territorio come soggetto corale*. Rome: Donzelli, 2015.

Becattini, G., M. Bellandi & L. De Propris (eds), *A Handbook of Industrial Districts*. Cheltenham: Elgar, 2009.

Bellandi, M. & A. Magnaghi (eds), *La coscienza di luogo nel recente pensiero di Giacomo Becattini*. Florence: Firenze University Press, 2017.

Benigno, F., "La questione delle origini: mafia, camorra e storia d'Italia", *Meridiana* 87 (2016), 125–47.

Berta, G., *Fiat Chrysler e la deriva dell'Italia industriale*. Bologna: Il Mulino, 2011.

Bourdieu, P., *Outline of a Theory of Practice*. Cambridge: Cambridge University Press, 1972.

Brandolini, A. & T. M. Smeeding, "Inequality Patterns in Western Democracies: Cross-Country Differences and Changes Over Time", in P. Beramendi & C. J. Anderson (eds), *Democracy, Inequality and Representation*, 25–61. New York: Russell Sage Foundation, 2008.

Bruni, L. & S. Zamagni, *Civil Economy*. Newcastle upon Tyne: Agenda, 2017.

Brusco, S., *Piccole imprese e distretti industriali*. Torino: Rosenberg & Sellier, 1989.

Cariati, V. *et al.*, *Storia delle società italiane di ingegneria e impiantistica*. Bologna: Il Mulino, 2012.

Charron, N., L. Dijkstra & V. Lapuente, "Mapping the Regional Divide in Europe: A Measure for Assessing Quality of Government in 2016 European Regions", *Social Indicators Research* 122 (2015), 315–46.

Ciocca, P., "Brigantaggio ed economia nel Mezzogiorno d'Italia, 1860–1870", *Rivista di Storia Economica* 29:1 (2013), 3–30.

Ciocca, P., 6. *L'IRI nell'economia italiana*. Bari: Laterza, 2014.

Clark, J., *Mondo Agnelli: Fiat, Chrysler and the Power of a Dynasty*. Chichester: Wiley, 2011.

Clô, A. (ed.), *ENI 1953–2003*. Bologna: Compositori, 2003.

Colli, A., *The History of Family Business 1850–2000*. Cambridge: Cambridge University Press, 2003.

Colli, A. & P. Fernandez Perez, *The Endurance of Large Family Businesses Around the World*. Cambridge: Cambridge University Press, 2013.

Coltorti, F., *Medie imprese del settore meccanico elettronico*. Available at: http://www.osservatoriodistretti.org/sites/default/files/le-medie-imprese-del-settore-meccanico-elettronico-2015.pdf (accessed 28 February 2018).

Coltorti, F. *et al.* (eds), *Mid-sized Manufacturing Companies: The New Driver of Italian Competitiveness*. Milan: Springer Verlag Italia, 2013.

De Blasio, G. & P. Sestito (eds), *Il capitale sociale. Che cos'è e cosa spiega*. Rome: Donzelli, 2011.

De Blasio, G. & G. Nuzzo, "Historical Traditions of Civicness and Local Economic Development", *Journal of Regional Science* 50 (2010), 833–57.

Di Nucci, L., *La democrazia distributiva. Saggio sul sistema politico dell'Italia repubblicana*. Bologna: Il Mulino, 2016.

Diaz del Hoyo *et al.*, "Real Convergence in the Euro Area: A Long-term Perspective", ECB Occasional Paper No. 203, December 2017.

Dickie, J., *Blood Brotherhoods: A History of Italy's Three Mafias*. New York: Public Affairs, 2014.

REFERENCES

European Central Bank, "Increasing Resilience and Long Term Growth: the Importance of Sound Institutions and Economic Structures for Euro Area Countries and EMU", *ECB Economic Bulletin* 5 (2016). Available at: https://www.ecb.europa.eu/pub/pdf/other/eb201605_article03.en.pdf (accessed 28 February 2018).

Fanfani, R., *Il sistema agroalimentare in Italia: i grandi cambiamenti e le tendenze recenti*. Milan: Ed agricole-Sole 24 ore, 2009.

Favero, G., *Benetton. I colori del successo*. Milan: Egea, 2005.

Felice, E., *Perchè il Sud è rimasto indietro*. Bologna: Il Mulino, 2013.

Felice, E., "Il divario Nord-Sud in Italia (1861–2011): lo stato dell'arte". MPRA paper no. 62209, February 2015.

Felice, E., "The Misty Grail: the Search for a Comprehensive Measure of Development and the Reasons for GDP Primacy", *Development and Change* 47:5 (2016), 967–94.

Felice, E. & M. Vasta, "Passive Modernization? The New Human Development Index and its Components in Italy's Regions (1871–2007)", *European Review of Economic History* 19:1 (2015), 44–66.

Fiocco, G., *L'Italia prima del miracolo economico. L'inchiesta parlamentare sulla miseria 1951–54*. Manduria: 2004.

Fiorino, N. & E. Galli, *La corruzione in Italia*. Bologna: Il Mulino, 2013.

Fortis, M., *The Pillars of the Italian Economy: Manufacturing, Food and Wine, Tourism*. Cham: Springer, 2016.

Fortis, M. & A. Quadrio Curzio, *Industria e distretti. Un paradigma di perdurante competitività italiana*. Bologna: Il Mulino, 2006.

Francese, M. & A. Pace, "Il debito pubblico italiano dall'Unità ad oggi. Una ricostruzione della serie storica". Bank of Italy paper no. 31, October 2008.

Fuà, G. & C. Zacchia (eds), *Industrializzazione senza fratture*. Bologna: Il Mulino, 1983.

Gambetta, D., *The Sicilian Mafia*. Cambridge, MA: Harvard University Press, 1996.

Garuzzo, G., *Fiat: The Secrets of an Epoch*. Cham: Springer, 2014.

Giacalone, D., *Razza corsara. Mercati mal controllati e la politica in fuga. Il caso Telecom e la mala privatizzazione*. Rubbettino, 2004.

Giannetti, R. & M. Vasta, "The concentration of the industrial structure, 1913–1971", in R. Giannetti & M. Vasta (eds), *Evolution of the Italian Enterprises in the Twentieth Century*. Heidelberg: Physica-Verlag, 2006.

Giannola, A., "Crisi del Mezzogiorno e nuove spinte migratorie", in I. Gjergji (ed.), *La nuova emigrazione. Cause, mete e figure sociali*, 39-56. Venice: Ca' Foscari, 2015.

Giordano, C. & F. Zollino, "A Historical Reconstruction of Capital and Labour in Italy, 1861–2013", *Rivista di Storia Economica* XXXI: 2 (2015).

Giunta, A. & S. Rossi, *Che cosa sa fare l'Italia. La nostra economia dopo la grande crisi.* Bari: Laterza, 2017.

Guidi, R., K. Fonović & T. Cappadozzi (eds), *Volontari e attività volontarie.* Bologna: Il Mulino, 2016.

Guiso, L., P. Sapienza & L. Zingales, "Civic Capital as the Missing Link", in J. Benhabib, A. Bisin & M. Jackson (eds), *Handbook of Social Economics*, Vol 1A, 417–80. San Diego: North Holland, 2011.

Kaufmann, D., A. Kraay & M. Mastruzzi, "The WGI: Methodology and Analytical Issues". Public Policy Working Paper no. 5430, World Bank, September 2010.

La Spina, A., *Mafia, legalità debole e sviluppo del Mezzogiorno.* Bologna: Il Mulino, 2005.

Lepre, A., *Storia della prima repubblica. L'Italia dal 1942 al 1992.* Bologna: Il Mulino, 1993.

Livi Bacci, M. (ed.), *Demografia del capitale umano.* Bologna: Il Mulino, 2010.

Lombardi, S. & G. Magliocchi, "Distretti industriali tra mutamento territoriale, economico e profili d'impresa", *L'Industria* 37:2 (2016), 329–61.

Macchiati, A., *Perchè l'Italia cresce poco.* Bologna: Il Mulino, 2016.

Magnani, M., *Terra e buoi dei paesi tuoi. Scuola, ricerca, ambiente, cultura, capitale umano: quando l'impresa investe nel territorio.* Novara: Utet, 2016.

Malanima, P., *Energy Consumption in Italy in the Nineteenth and Twentieth Centuries.* Naples: CNR, 2006.

Masuch, K., E. Moshammer & B. Pierluigi, "Institutions, Public Debt and Growth in Europe". ECB working paper no. 1963, September 2016.

Mattesini, F. & M. Messori, *L'evoluzione del Sistema bancario meridionale.* Bologna: Il Mulino, 2004.

Ministry of Economic Development (MISE), *La situazione energetica nazionale nel 2016,* April 2017.

Muzzarelli, M., *Breve storia della moda in Italia.* Bologna: Il Mulino, 2011.

Nifo, A. & G. Vecchione, "Do Institutions Play a Role in Skilled Migration? The Case of Italy", *Regional Studies* 48 (2014), 1628–49.

Nuzzo, G., "Un secolo di statistiche sociali: persistenza o convergenza delle regioni italiane?", *Quaderni dell'Ufficio Ricerche Storiche della Banca d'Italia*, no.11, 2006.

Omiccioli, M. (ed.), *I sistemi produttivi locali. Trasformazioni fra globalizzazione e crisi.* Rome: Carocci, 2013.

REFERENCES

Onida, F., *Se il piccolo non cresce. Piccole e medie imprese italiane in affanno.* Bologna, Il Mulino, 2004.

Perrotta, C. & C. Sunna (eds), *L'arretratezza del Mezzogiorno. Le idee, l'economia, la storia.* Milan: Bruno Mondadori, 2012.

Piluso, G., *Mediobanca tra regole e mercato.* Milan: Egea, 2005.

Prometeia, *L'economia della bellezza. Quanto vale e qual è il suo potenziale.* Online manuscript, 2017. Available at http://www.upa.it/static/upload/eco/economiadellabellezzaricercacompleta.pdf (accessed 27 June 2018).

Pugliese, E., *L'Italia tra migrazioni internazionali e migrazioni interne.* Bologna: Il Mulino, 2006.

Pugliese, E., *La terza età. Anziani e società in Italia.* Bologna: Il Mulino, 2011.

Putnam, R., *Making Democracy Work.* Princeton, NJ: Princeton University Press, 1993.

Russolillo, F. (ed.), *5. Un gruppo singolare. Settori, bilanci, presenza nell'economia italiana.* Bari: Laterza, 2014.

Salvini S. & A. De Rose (eds), *Rapporto sulla popolazione. L'Italia a 150 anni dall'Unità.* Bologna: Il Mulino, 2011.

Sanna, F. & V. De Bernardo (eds), *Sviluppo locale e cooperazione sociale.* Rome: Ecra, 2015.

Saviano, R., *Gomorrah.* London: Picador, 2006.

Savona, E. & M. Riccardi (eds), *From Illegal Markets to Legitimate Businesses: The Portfolio of Organized Crime in Europe.* Trento: Transcrime, 2015.

Toninelli, P., "Energy and the Puzzle of Italy's Economic Growth", *Journal of Modern Italian Studies* 15:1 (2010), 107–27.

Toth, F., *La sanità in Italia.* Bologna: Il Mulino, 2014.

Traclò, F. & W. Tortorella, *Oltre i limiti del turismo all'italiana.* Bologna: Il Mulino, 2007.

Turani, G., *I sogni del grande Nord.* Bologna: Il Mulino, 1996.

Varini, V., "Il welfare aziendale in Italia. Dalla storiografia a un caso di studio", in P. Battilani & C. Benassi (eds), *Consumare il welfare. L'esperienzaitaliana del secondo Novecento*, 77–110. Bologna, Il Mulino, 2013.

Vecchi, G., *In ricchezza e in povertà. Il benessere degli Italiani dall'Unità ad oggi.* Bologna: Il Mulino, 2011.

Venturi, P. & S. Rago (eds), *Ri-Generare le Istituzioni. Il contributo dell'Economia Civile all'Innovazione istituzionale.* Forlì: Aiccon, 2014.

Zamagni, S. & V. Zamagni, *Famiglia e lavoro. Opposizione o armonia?* Turin: San Paolo, 2012.

Zamagni, V., *The Economic History of Italy 1860–1990*. Oxford: Clarendon Press, 1993.

Zamagni, V., "L'offerta di istruzione in Italia 1861–1981", in G. Gili, M. Lupo & I. Zilli (eds), *Scuola e società. Le istituzioni scolastiche in Italia dall'età moderna al futuro*, 143–82. Naples: ESI, 2002.

Zamagni, V., *Italcementi. Dalla leadership nazionale all'internazionalizzazione*. Bologna: Il Mulino, 2006.

Zamagni, V., *Finmeccanica. Competenze che vengono da lontano*. Bologna: Il Mulino, 2009.

Zamagni, V., *L'industria chimica italiana e l'IMI*. Bologna: Il Mulino, 2010.

Zamagni, V., "La situazione economico-sociale del Mezzogiorno negli anni dell'unificazione", *Meridiana* 73/74 (2012), 267–81.

Zamagni, V., *Come si è affermata la grande impresa cooperativa in Italia. Il contributo di Enea Mazzoli*. Bologna: Il Mulino, 2015.

Zamagni, V., "The Cooperative Movement", in E. Jones & G. Pasquino (eds), *The Oxford Handbook of Italian Politics*. Oxford: Oxford University Press, 2015.

Zamagni, V., "L'industria chimica", in A. Gigliobianco & G. Toniolo (eds), *Concorrenza, mercato e crescita in Italia: il lungo periodo*, 351–86. Venice: Marsilio, 2017.

Zamagni, V., *An Economic History of Europe Since 1700*. Newcastle upon Tyne: Agenda Publishing, 2017.

Index